Thirteer

THE TEXAS NOTARY LAW PRIMER

*All the hard-to-find information
every Texas Notary Public
needs to know!*

National Notary Association

Published by:

National Notary Association
9350 De Soto Ave.
Chatsworth, CA 91311-4926
Telephone: (818) 739-4000
Fax: (818) 700-0920
Website: www.NationalNotary.org
Email: nna@nationalnotary.org

The information in this *Primer* is correct and current at the time
of its publication, although new laws, regulations and rulings may
subsequently affect the validity of certain sections. This information
is provided to aid comprehension of state Notary Public requirements
and should not be construed as legal advice. Please consult an
attorney for inquiries relating to legal matters.

Thirteenth Edition © 2011
First Edition © 1980

ISBN: 978-1-59767-089-0

Table of Contents

For the latest updates on state laws
and requirements, please visit

NationalNotary.org/Primer-Updates

Have a Tough Notary Question?

If you were an NNA member, you could get the answer to that
difficult question. Join the NNA and your membership includes
access to the Notary Hotline* and live Notary experts providing the
latest Notary information regarding laws, rules and regulations.

Hours

Monday – Friday   5:00 a.m. – 7:00 p.m. (PST)

Saturdays   5:00 a.m. – 5:00 p.m. (PST)

Hotline Toll-Free Phone Number: 1-888-876-0827

After hours you can leave a message or email our experts at
Hotline@NationalNotary.org and they will respond the next business day.

*Access to the Notary Hotline is for NNA members only. Call and become a
member today.

Introduction

We commend you on your interest in Texas Notary law. Purchasing *The Texas Notary Law Primer* identifies you as a conscientious professional who takes your official responsibilities seriously.

In few fields is the expression "more to it than meets the eye" truer than in Notary law. What often appears on the surface to be a simple procedure may, in fact, have important legal implications.

The purpose of *The Texas Notary Law Primer* is to provide you with a resource to help decipher the many intricate laws that affect notarization. The *Primer* will acquaint you with all important aspects of Texas Notary law and with prudent notarial practices in general.

This thirteenth edition includes changes effective September 1, 2011 allowing Notaries to accept a current foreign passport as satisfactory evidence of identity for deeds or other instruments related to residential real estate transactions only.

While *The Texas Notary Law Primer* begins with informative chapters on how to obtain your commission, what tools you need, commonly-asked questions, and the critical steps for performing a notarization, the heart of this book is the chapter entitled "Notary Laws Explained." In that chapter, we explain the myriad Notary laws and put them in easy-to-understand terms. Every pertinent section of the law is analyzed and explained, as well as topics not covered by Texas law but nonetheless of vital concern to you as a Notary.

For handy reference, we have reprinted the complete text of the laws of Texas that relate to the duties of Notaries Public. In addition, we have included addresses and phone numbers of the Secretary of State's office, Texas County Clerk offices and Bureaus of Vital Statistics, plus a list of nations that are parties to the Hague Convention, a treaty that simplifies the process of authentication.

Whether you're about to be commissioned for the first time, or a long-time Notary, we are sure *The Texas Notary Law Primer* will provide you with new insights and understanding. Your improved comprehension of Texas Notary law will naturally result in greater competence as a professional Notary Public.

> Milton G. Valera
> Chairman
> National Notary Association

How to Become a Texas Notary Public

1. Ensure that you comply with the basic qualifications for a Texas Notary commission.

First, you must be a legal resident of the state; however, an escrow agent who is a resident of a state adjacent to Texas and who is an attorney, or an escrow agent who is an employee of a title insurance agent or direct operation with an office in Texas, may become a Texas Notary. Second, you must be 18 years of age or older. And third, you must not have been convicted of a felony or any crime involving moral turpitude.

U.S. citizenship is not required as long as you legally reside in this country under federal law. A minimum time of state residency is not required; you can apply for a commission on the same day you enter Texas.

2. Obtain a commission application form.

The official application for a Texas Notary commission is available from the Secretary of State by calling (512) 463-5705 or in person or by mail through the addresses below. Applications are also available online at www.sos.state.tx.us/statdoc/forms/2301.pdf. If you are renewing your current Notary commission, request an application for reappointment from the same office. The renewal application will not automatically be sent upon expiration.

Street Address:
Secretary of State
Notary Public Unit
1019 Brazos
Austin, TX 78701

Mailing Address:
Secretary of State
Notary Public Unit
P.O. Box 13375
Austin, TX 78711-3375

3. Complete the application form.

Fill out the application, typing or printing neatly in ink. Be aware that any misstatement or omission of requested information is cause for denial or later revocation of a Notary commission.

4. Purchase your Notary bond.

The Notary application will include a surety bond form. Take or mail this form to a licensed surety company and purchase a $10,000 Notary bond.

If you are employed by an agency of the state of Texas, you might not be required to obtain a Notary surety bond — discuss this with your governmental employer.

5. Submit the application with the commission fees and your Notary bond.

The completed and signed application must be mailed or delivered to the Secretary of State's Notary Public Unit at the address on page 3. A $21 fee — payable to "Secretary of State" — and the surety bond must be enclosed with the application.

If you are renewing your Notary appointment, the application must be submitted no earlier than 90 days before your current appointment expires. However, if the application is submitted past the expiration date, there will be no grace period allowing you to notarize during the gap between appointments.

6. Take and sign your oath of office.

Once your application has been approved, the Secretary of State will send you your official Notary commission. On the commission is the official oath of office, which must be signed and executed before an officer authorized to administer oaths — a Notary Public, for example, but not yourself. Although you must take an oath of office, the oath itself is not required to be filed with the Secretary of State.

7. Obtain an official Notary seal and journal.

Before you perform any notarial act with your new Notary commission, you must obtain an official seal of office and an official journal of notarial acts. See "Notary Seal" on pages 50–51 for the specific requirements of Texas law regarding a Notary seal.

In addition, you also must obtain or make a schedule of the maximum fees that Texas statute allows Notaries to charge. This schedule must be posted in a conspicuous place in the office where you will notarize. ∎

Tools
of the Trade

Notaries need several tools to carry out their duties lawfully and efficiently. These tools are as important to the Notary as a hammer and saw are to the carpenter.

Inking Seal

The inked rubber seal affixes a photographically reproducible impression in indelible ink. It is a convenient official seal for notarizing deeds and other documents that will be submitted to a public recorder for microfilming. The Notary's seal must include the words "Notary Public, State of Texas" around a five-point star, the Notary's name, and the expiration date of the Notary's commission.

Seal Embosser

The embosser may be used by itself as an official Texas Notary seal; however, when an embosser is affixed on documents that will be publicly recorded and microfilmed (deeds, etc.), the resulting impression must be smudged with ink, graphite, or carbon to become photographically reproducible. Many Notaries use an embosser as a fraud deterrent in addition to an inking seal; embossing pages and certificates together deters their fraudulent replacement. Because photocopies of documents can easily pass as originals today, the embossment can be used to distinguish an original from a photocopy. When used in conjunction with an inking seal, the embossment does not have to be smudged.

Journal of Notarial Acts

The Notary is required by law to keep a journal record of every document notarized. The journal record must include the date of the document, the date of the notarization, the name and residence of the parties whose signatures are being notarized, the type of information used to verify the identity of the signers and a brief description of the document. The Notary's journal provides a record of notarial transactions that may be used as evidence in a court proceeding.

Jurat Stamp

The jurat stamp impresses on a document the jurat wording "Subscribed and sworn to before me this _____ day of _____, _____ by _____." The jurat stamp is more convenient (and safer, since critical wording will not be omitted) than typing the wording on each document that requires it.

Venue Stamp

The venue stamp is used in conjunction with the jurat stamp in a jurat. The phrase, "State of _____, County of _____," indicates where the notarization was executed. It may also be used for acknowledgments.

Notarial Certificates

Preprinted notarial certificates for acknowledgments, jurats, proofs of execution by subscribing witness, and copy certification by document custodian are available.

Errors and Omissions Insurance

Notary errors and omissions (E&O) insurance provides protection for Notaries who are sued for damages resulting from unintentional notarial mistakes. In the event of a lawsuit, the E&O insurance company will provide and pay for the Notary's legal counsel and absorb any damages levied by a court or agreed to in a settlement, up to the policy coverage limit. E&O insurance does not cover the Notary for intentional misconduct. ■

As a full-service organization, the National Notary Association makes available to Texas Notaries all notarial items required by law, custom and convenience.

10 Most-Asked Questions

Every Notary has a question or two about whether and how to notarize. But certain questions pop up again and again. These top 10 are asked repeatedly at the National Notary Association's seminars, its annual National Conference of Notaries Public, and through its Notary Hotline.

As with most questions about notarization, the answer to these 10 is not always a simple "yes" or "no." Rather, the answer is, "It depends."

Here's what every Notary wants to know:

1. Can I notarize a will?

It depends. A Notary should notarize a will only if clear instructions and a notarial certificate are provided. If the signer of the will is relying upon the Notary for advice on how to proceed, the Notary should tell the individual to consult an attorney.

Laws regarding wills differ from state to state. Some states do not require notarization of wills, while others allow it as one of several witnessing options. Often it is not the will itself that is notarized, but accompanying affidavits signed by witnesses.

The danger in notarizing wills is that would-be testators who have drafted their own wills without legal advice may believe that notarization will make their wills legal and valid. However, even when notarized, such homemade wills may be worthless because the testators failed to obtain the proper number of witnesses or omitted important information.

In fact, notarization itself may actually void an otherwise properly executed handwritten (holographic) will, because courts have occasionally held that any writing on the document other than the testator's invalidates the will.

2. Can I notarize for a stranger with no identification?

Yes. If identification of a signer cannot be based on personal knowledge or identification documents (ID cards), a Notary may rely upon the oath or affirmation of one credible identifying witness to identify an unknown signer.

The Notary must know the credible identifying witness personally, who must know the document signer personally. This establishes a chain of personal knowledge from the Notary to the credible identifying witness to the signer.

A credible identifying witness should be someone the Notary believes to be trustworthy and impartial. If a person has a financial or other beneficial interest in a document, that individual could not be a reliable witness.

When no credible identifying witness is available to identify a stranger without IDs, the Notary may have no choice but to tell the signer to find a personally known Notary or a friend who personally knows a Notary.

3. Can I notarize a photograph?

No. To simply stamp and sign a photograph is improper. A Notary's signature and seal must appear only on a notarial certificate (such as an acknowledgment or jurat) accompanying a written statement signed by another person.

However, a signature on a written statement referring to an accompanying or attached photograph may be notarized; if the photograph is large enough, the statement and notarial certificate might even appear on its reverse side. Such a format may be acceptable when notarized photos are requested by persons seeking medical or health licenses, or by legal resident aliens renewing foreign passports.

A word of caution here: a Notary should always be suspicious about notarizing a photo-bearing card or document that could be used as a bogus "official" ID.

4. What if there's no room for my seal or if it smears?

Usually, if notarial wording printed on a document leaves no room for a seal, a loose certificate can be attached and filled out instead, if the certificate wording is substantially the same as on the document.

If an initial seal impression is unreadable and there is ample room on the document, another impression can be affixed nearby. The illegibility of the first impression will indicate why a second seal impression was necessary. The Notary should record in the journal that a second seal was applied.

A Notary never should attempt to fix an imperfect seal impression with pen, ink, or correction fluid. This may be viewed as evidence of tampering and cause the document's rejection by a recorder.

5. Can I notarize signatures on photocopies of documents?

Yes. A photocopy may be notarized as long as it bears an original signature, meaning that the photocopy must have been signed with pen and ink. A photocopied signature may never be notarized.

Note that some public recorders may not accept notarized signatures on photocopied sheets because they will not adequately reproduce in microfilming.

When carbon copies are made, the Notary will sometimes be asked to conform rather than to notarize the copies. To conform a copy, the Notary reaffixes the official seal on the copy (carbon will not readily transfer a seal impression) and writes "Conformed Copy" prominently across the top of the copy.

6. May I notarize for customers only?

No. As a public official, a Notary is not commissioned to serve just the customers or clients of any one business, even when the Notary's employer has paid for the bond, commissioning fees, and notarial supplies. There is no such officer as a "Notary Private."

It is ethically improper — although hardly ever explicitly prohibited by statute — to discriminate between customers and noncustomers in offering or refusing to offer notarial services and in charging or not charging fees.

Discrimination against anyone who presents a lawful request for notarization is not a suitable policy for a public official commissioned to serve all of the public equally. Also, such discrimination can provide the basis for lawsuits.

7. Can I notarize a document in a language I can't read?

Yes. As long as the notarial certificate and document signature are in a language the Notary can read, Texas Notaries may notarize documents written in a language they cannot read.

However, there are certain difficulties and dangers in doing so. The main difficulty for the Notary is making an accurate journal description of an unreadable document. The main danger is that the document may be blatantly fraudulent.

Under no circumstances should a notarization be performed if the Notary and the principal signer cannot communicate in the same language.

8. Can I certify a copy of a birth certificate?

No. While Texas Notaries are authorized to certify copies, they are specifically prohibited from certifying copies of documents that are either public records or publicly recordable.

Only an officer in a bureau of vital statistics should certify a copy of a birth certificate or other vital public record; a Notary's "certification" of a birth or death record may actually lend credibility to a counterfeit or tampered document. Only a county recording official should certify a copy of a deed or other recordable instrument.

The types of documents that Texas Notaries may properly certify copies of are original personal papers such as letters and in-house business documents.

9. Does a document have to be signed in my presence?

It depends. Documents requiring acknowledgments normally do not need to be signed in the Notary's presence. However, the signer must appear before the Notary at the time of notarization to acknowledge that he or she freely signed for the purposes stated in the document.

An acknowledgment certificate indicates that the signer personally appeared before the Notary, was identified by the Notary, and acknowledged to the Notary that the document was freely signed.

On the other hand, documents requiring a jurat must be signed in the Notary's presence, as dictated by the typical jurat wording, "Subscribed (signed) and sworn to before me...."

In executing a jurat, a Notary guarantees the signer personally appeared before the Notary, was given an oath or affirmation by the Notary, and signed in the Notary's presence. In addition, even though it may not be a statutory requirement that the Notary positively identify a signer for a jurat, it is always a good idea to do so.

10. Can I notarize for a family member?

It depends. Although state law does not directly address notarizing for family members, the Secretary of State advises that a Notary should not notarize in these cases. Notaries who do so may violate the statutes prohibiting a direct beneficial interest — especially in notarizing for spouses in states, such as Texas, with community property laws.

Besides the possibility of a financial interest in notarizing for a relative, there may be an "emotional interest" that can prevent the Notary from acting impartially. For example, a Notary who is asked to notarize a contract signed by his brother might attempt to persuade the sibling to sign or not sign. As a brother, the individual is entitled to exert influence — but this is entirely improper for a Notary.

Even if a Notary has no direct beneficial interest in the document and does not attempt to influence the signer, notarizing for a relative could subject the document to a legal challenge if other parties to the transaction allege that the Notary could not have acted impartially. ■

Steps to Proper Notarization

When Notaries perform a notarial act, they are expected to exercise what is known as "reasonable care." Reasonable care is the level of precaution expected of a person of ordinary prudence and intelligence.

The first rule of reasonable care is strict adherence to all laws governing Notaries and notarization. In situations not explicitly covered by statute, the Notary should make every effort to use common sense and behave in a responsible fashion.

A Notary who fails to exercise reasonable care may be subject to a civil suit to recover financial damages resulting from the Notary's error. If a Notary can convincingly show that he or she used reasonable care when performing a notarization, on the other hand, that will help shield the Notary from liability in the event that the notarization is challenged.

The following 14-step checklist will help Notaries to apply the principles associated with reasonable care and to avoid the most common pitfalls associated with notarization. Always following these guidelines will help protect the Notary in the event of a civil suit.

1. Require every signer to personally appear.

The signer must appear in person before the Notary on the date and in the county stated in the notarial certificate. "Personal appearance" means the signer is in the Notary's physical presence — face to face in the same room. A telephone call is not acceptable in lieu of personal appearance.

2. Make a careful identification.

The Notary should identify every document signer through either personal knowledge, the oath of a credible identifying witness, or through reliable identification documents (ID cards).

When using ID cards, the Notary must examine them closely to detect alteration, counterfeiting, or evidence that they are issued to an impostor. Do not rely on a type of card with which you are unfamiliar, unless you check it against a reference such as the *U.S. Identification Manual* or the *ID Checking Guide*.

3. Feel certain the signer is aware.

A conscientious and careful Notary will be certain not only of the signer's identity and willingness to sign, but will also make a layperson's judgment about the signer's ability to understand the document and to be aware of its import.

While Texas law does not expressly require the Notary to make a judgment about awareness, it is in the Notary's best interest to do so. A document signer who is not able to respond intelligibly in a simple conversation with the Notary should be considered unaware and unable to sign at that moment.

If in doubt, the Notary can ask the signer if he or she understands the document and can explain its purpose. Or, if the notarization is to be performed in a medical environment while the signer is under medical care, the signer's doctor can be consulted for a professional opinion.

4. Check the signature.

The Notary must make sure the document signer signs the same name appearing on the identification presented.

To check for possible forgery, the Notary should compare the signature the person leaves in the journal of notarial acts against the signatures on the document and on the IDs. Also, it should be noted whether the signer appears to be laboring on the journal signature, a possible indication of forgery in progress. (While Texas law does not require the document signer to also sign the Notary's journal, prudent Notaries always will ask for a journal signature.)

In certain circumstances, it may be acceptable to make allowances for a signer who is signing with an abbreviated form of his or her name (John D. Smith instead of John David Smith), as long as the individual is signing with less than and not more than what is on the identification document.

5. Look for blank spaces.

Although not expressly prohibited by Texas law, notarization of incomplete documents is an unwise practice.

Documents with blank spaces have a great potential for fraud. A borrower, for example, might sign an incomplete promissory note, trusting the lender to fill it out, and then later find that the lender has written in an amount in excess of what was actually borrowed.

If the blanks are inapplicable and intended to be left unfilled, the signer may be asked to line through each space (using ink), or to write in "Not Applicable" or "N/A."

6. Scan the document.

Notaries are not required to read the documents they notarize. However, they should note certain important particulars about a document, such as its title, for recording in the journal of notarial acts. Notaries must be sure to count and record the number of pages; this can show whether pages are later fraudulently added or removed.

7. Check the document's date.

For acknowledgments, the date of signing on the document should either precede or be the same as the date of the notarization; it should not follow it. For a jurat, the document signing date and the notarization date must be the same.

A document dated to follow the date on its notarial certificate risks rejection by a recorder, who may question how the document could have been notarized before it was signed.

8. Keep a journal of notarial acts.

A journal is mandatory for all Notaries in Texas. If a notarized document is lost or altered, or if certain facts about the transaction are later challenged, the Notary's journal becomes valuable evidence. It can protect the rights of all parties to a transaction and help Notaries defend themselves against false accusations.

The Notary should include all the pertinent details of the notarization in the journal, such as the date and type of notarization, the date and type of document, the name and address of the signer, how this person was identified and notarial fees charged, if any. In addition, any other pertinent data, such as the representative capacity the signer is claiming, may be entered. Signers may also be asked to leave a signature in the Notary's journal as a deterrent to fraud, although this is not required by law in Texas.

STEPS TO PROPER NOTARIZATION

9. Complete the journal entry first.

The Notary should complete the journal entry entirely before filling out the notarial certificate. This prevents a signer from leaving before the important public record of the notarization is made in the journal.

10. Make sure the document has notarial wording.

If a notarial certificate does not come with the document, the Notary must ask the document signer what type of notarization — acknowledgment, jurat or other — is required. The Notary then may type the appropriate notarial wording on the document or attach a preprinted, loose certificate.

If the signer does not know what type of notarization is required, he or she should contact the document's issuing or receiving agency to determine the type of notarization needed. This decision is never the Notary's to make unless the Notary is also an attorney.

11. Be attentive to details.

When filling out the certificate, the Notary needs to make sure the venue correctly identifies the place of notarization. If the venue is preprinted and incorrect, the Notary must line through the incorrect state and/or county, write in the proper site of the notarization, and initial and date the change.

Also, the Notary must pay attention to spaces on the notarial certificate that indicate the number and gender of the document signers, as well as how they were identified — for example, leave the plural "(s)" in "person(s)" untouched or cross it out, as appropriate.

12. Affix your signature and seal properly.

Notaries should sign exactly the same name appearing on their commissioning papers. They also must affix an official seal — a common reason for rejection of a document by a recorder.

The seal should be placed as close to the Notary's signature as possible without overprinting it. To prevent illegibility, a Notary seal should not be affixed over wording, particularly over a signature. Although an embossment may be placed over the letters "L.S.," an inked seal impression should be affixed next to but not over them to ensure legibility of data in the seal.

15

13. Protect loose certificates.

If the Notary has to attach a notarial certificate, it should be securely stapled to the left margin of the document. Notaries can protect against the removal of such loose certificates by embossing them together with the documents and writing the particulars of the document to which the certificate is attached in one of the certificate's margins. For example, the notation, "This certificate is attached to a 15-page partnership agreement between John Smith and Mary Doe, signed July 14, 2009," would deter fraudulent removal and reattachment of a loose certificate.

14. Don't give advice.

Every state prohibits nonattorneys from practicing law. Notaries should never prepare or complete documents for others, nor give advice on any matter relating to a document unless they are attorneys or professionals certified or licensed in a relevant area of expertise. The nonattorney Notary never chooses the type of certificate or notarization a document needs, since this decision can have important legal ramifications. The Notary could be held liable for any damages resulting from an incorrectly chosen certificate or notarization. ■

Notary Laws Explained

In layperson's language, this chapter discusses and clarifies key parts of the laws of Texas that regulate Notaries Public. Most of these laws are reprinted in full in "Texas Laws Pertaining to Notaries Public," beginning on page 75.

This edition explains the new laws, effective September 1, 2009, that clarify the judicial actions that may not be used to reject an application for a Notary commission or to suspend or revoke the commission of a Notary and permit advance directives, including do-not-resuscitate (DNR) orders and medical powers of attorney, to be signed before either two witnesses or a Notary and permits these documents to be signed and notarized electronically using an electronic or digital signature.

In the text that follows, these abbreviations are used:

TAC — Texas Administrative Code, which contains administrative regulations implementing specific statutes.

TGC — Texas Government Code, which contains most of the laws regulating the activities of Notaries Public.

TCPRC — Texas Civil Practices and Remedies Code, which sets rules for the taking of acknowledgments and proofs of written instruments.

TIC — Texas Insurance Code.

NPEM — *Notary Public Educational Materials*, issued to newly commissioned Notaries Public by the Secretary of State.

THE NOTARY COMMISSION

Application for Commission

Qualifications. To become a Notary in Texas, the applicant must meet the following qualifications (TGC, Sec. 406.004):

- Be at least 18 years old

- Be a legal resident of Texas

- Not have been convicted of a felony or any crime involving moral turpitude

In addition, the applicant must properly complete and submit the Notary application, obtain a $10,000 bond (see "Notary Bond," below), and pay all required fees (see "Application Fee," following). Once commissioned, the Notary also must take and sign the oath of office (TGC, Sec. 406.006).

Nonresident Escrow Agents. The following nonresidents may qualify for a Texas Notary commission without meeting the Texas residency requirements (TIC 2652.051):

- Escrow agents who are residents of a state adjacent to Texas and who are attorneys

- Escrow agents who are employees of a title insurance agent or direct operation with an office in Texas

Application Fee. The total fee for a Notary commission applicant is $21. This includes $10 for approving and filing the bond, $10 for the commission itself, and $1 for the Secretary of State to employ an investigator and to prepare and distribute commissioning materials (TGC, Sec. 406.007).

Rejection of Application. The Secretary of State may reject a Notary application for any of the following (TGC, Sec. 406.009):

- A false statement knowingly made in the application

- A conviction for a felony or a crime involving moral turpitude

- An imposition of an administrative, criminal, or civil penalty or a conviction for a violation of Notary law in any state

- Failure to comply with Texas Government Code, Section 406.017, regarding false advertising, misrepresentation, and illegal translation of the words "Notary Public" into Spanish

- Performing a notarization without requiring personal appearance of the signer

Reappointment. A Notary may not apply to renew his or her commission earlier than 90 days before the expiration of the Notary's current commission (TGC, Sec. 406.011).

Notary Bond

Requirement. Every Texas Notary is required to obtain a bond of $10,000 and submit it with the Notary application (TGC, Sec. 406.010). Employees of state agencies may not need to be bonded, depending on agency policy (TGC, 653.002 - 653.004).

The Notary bond must be purchased from a surety company authorized to do business in the state. The bond must be approved by the Secretary of State, payable to the Governor, and conditioned to provide reimbursement to any person damaged by the Notary's improper performance of official duties (TGC, Sec. 406.010).

Filing the Bond. The bond must be submitted with the Notary commission application at the office of the Secretary of State — before the applicant begins the official duties of office. The Secretary of State may accept an electronic filing of the bond per agreement with the surety firm (TGC, Sec. 406.010).

Protects Public. The Notary bond protects the public from a Notary's misconduct or negligence. The bond does not protect the Notary, who is personally liable for all damages resulting from illegal or improper performance of notarial duties (NPEM).

The bond's surety company agrees to pay damages totaling up to $10,000 to persons who suffer financially because of the Notary's improper acts, intentional or not, in the event the Notary does not have the financial resources to pay these damages. The surety may seek compensation from the Notary for any damages it has to pay out on the Notary's behalf.

Statement of Officer

Requirement. Each prospective Notary must take and sign a statement of officer in the presence of a Notary Public or other person authorized to administer oaths in Texas. This is the oath required by Section 1, Article XVI of the Texas Constitution. A Notary cannot execute his or her own statement of officer (TGC, Sec. 406.010).

Filing the Statement. The statement of officer appears on the Notary commission and is filed with the Secretary of State (TGC, Sec. 406.005).

Jurisdiction

Statewide. Notaries may perform official acts throughout the state of Texas but not beyond the state borders. A Notary may not witness a signing outside Texas and then return to the state to perform the notarization; all parts of a notarial act must be performed at the same time and place within the state of Texas (TGC, Sec. 406.003).

Term of Office

Four-Year Term. A Texas Notary Public's term of office is four years, ending at midnight on the commission expiration date (TGC, Sec. 406.002).

Resignation

Procedure. To resign, a Notary must deliver his or her journal and public papers to the county clerk in the county in which the Notary resides (TGC, Sec. 406.022).

The National Notary Association recommends the Notary also immediately notify the Secretary of State by certified mail and destroy his or her Notary seal. (See "Disposition of Notary Records," page 48.)

Change of Address

Notify Secretary of State. Whenever a Notary changes his or her address, the Notary must inform the Secretary of State of the address change within 10 days after the change (TGC, Sec. 406.019).

Moving Out of State. If a Notary moves his or her residence out of Texas, he or she vacates the office of Notary. Such a move has the same effect as resignation (see "Resignation," page 20) (TGC, Sec. 406.020).

Ex Officio Notaries. An ex officio Notary — one who acquires notarial powers because of a particular office or position — who moves permanently from his or her assigned jurisdiction vacates the office of Notary Public. Such a move has the same effect as resignation (see "Resignation," page 20) (TGC, Sec. 406.021).

Change of Name

Procedure. A Notary may change the name on his or her Notary Public commission by submitting the following to the Secretary of State (NPEM):

- A new application

- The original Notary commission

- A rider or endorsement from the bond agency or surety

- A $20 filing fee.

All four of these items must be sent at the same time. Instructions are available from the Notary Public Unit at (512) 463-5705.

Exception. Texas law does not require Notaries to change the name on their current commission in the event they change their name due to marriage or other reason. But the Notary must continue to use the name on the current commission for all official acts and then change the commission name when he or she renews.

OFFICIAL NOTARIAL ACTS

Authorized Acts

Notaries may perform the following official acts (TGC, Sec. 406.016 and TCPRC, Sec. 121.001):

- Acknowledgments, certifying that a signer personally appeared before the Notary, was identified by the Notary, and acknowledged freely signing the document. (See pages 23–27.)

- Certified Copies, guaranteeing that a photocopy of an original document not recordable in public records is true and complete. (See pages 27–31.)

- Depositions, certifying that the spoken words of a witness were accurately taken down in writing, though this act is most often done by skilled court reporters. (See pages 31–33.)

- Jurats, certifying that a signer personally appeared before the Notary, took an oath or affirmation from the Notary, and signed the document in the Notary's presence. (See pages 33–34.)

- Oaths and Affirmations, which are solemn promises to God (oaths) or solemn promises on one's own personal honor (affirmations). (See pages 34–36.)

- Proofs of Acknowledgment by Handwriting, in which witnesses appear before the Notary and swear to a deposition or affidavit that the signature of another person, the principal, is genuine. (See pages 36–38.)

- Proofs of Acknowledgment (or Execution) by Subscribing Witness, in which a subscribing witness personally appears and swears to the Notary that another person, the principal, signed a document willingly. (See pages 38–40.)

- Protests, certifying that a negotiable instrument or other written promise to pay, such as a bill of exchange, was not honored. (See pages 40–41.)

Unauthorized Acts

Notary's Own Signature. Notaries are not permitted to notarize their own signatures (NPEM).

Issue Identification. Notaries are not permitted to issue an identification card (TGC, Sec. 406.016).

Marriages. Texas Notaries are not authorized to perform marriages unless the Notary is also a member of the clergy or an official authorized to solemnize marriages.

Telephone Notarizations. Notarizations over the telephone are absolutely forbidden. A document signer must appear before the Notary, face to face in the same room, at the time of notarization, not before, not later (NPEM).

In addition, notarization based on a Notary's recognition of a signature, or on the unsworn word of a third party, without the signer's appearance before the Notary is forbidden (TGC, Sec. 406.009).

However, the sworn word of witnesses to the signing or acknowledging, or of persons who can identify the signature by handwriting, is permitted in special circumstances. (See "Proof of Acknowledgment by Handwriting," pages 36–38, and "Proof of Acknowledgment by Subscribing Witness," pages 38–40.)

Acknowledgments

A Common Notarial Act. Acknowledgments are one of the most common forms of notarization. Typically, they are executed on documents such as deeds and other documents affecting real property that will be publicly filed with a county recorder.

Purpose. In executing an acknowledgment, the Notary certifies three things (TCPRC, Secs. 121.005 and 121.006):

- The signer personally appeared before the Notary on the date and in the county indicated on the notarial certificate (notarization cannot be based on a telephone call or on a Notary's familiarity with a signature).

- The signer was positively identified by the Notary through personal knowledge or other satisfactory evidence (see "Identifying Document Signers," *et seq.*, pages 41–46).

- The signer acknowledged to the Notary that the signature was freely made for the purposes stated in the document. (If a document is willingly signed in the presence of the Notary, this tacit act can serve just as well as an oral statement of acknowledgment.)

Certificates for Acknowledgments. Texas law provides wording for an ordinary certificate of acknowledgment plus several short-form acknowledgment certificates that accommodate signers in various representative capacities and may be used as alternatives to other authorized certificates (TCPRC, Secs. 121.007 and 121.008).

- Ordinary Certificate of Acknowledgment — wording must be substantially as follows:

State of Texas   )

) ss.

County of   )

Before me _____ (name and title of officer) on this day personally appeared _____ (name[s] of signer[s]), known to me (or proved to me on the oath of _____ or through _____ [type of identification document]) to be the person(s) whose name(s) is/are subscribed to the foregoing instrument and acknowledged to me that he/she/they executed the same for the purposes and consideration therein expressed.

Given under my hand and seal of office this _____ day of _____, _____ (year).

_____ (Signature of Notary)   (Seal of Notary)

- Individual Acknowledgment Short-Form Certificate — for an individual or individuals signing on his, her or their own behalf:

State of Texas   )

) ss.

County of   )

This instrument was acknowledged before me on _____ (date) by _____ (name of signer[s]).

_____ (Signature of Notary)   (Seal of Notary)

- Attorney-in-Fact Acknowledgment Short-Form Certificate — for an attorney-in-fact acting on behalf of a principal:

State of Texas   )

) ss.

County of   )

This instrument was acknowledged before me on _____ (date) by _____ (name of attorney in fact) as attorney in fact for _____ (name of principal).

_____ (Signature of Notary)   (Seal of Notary)

- Partnership Acknowledgment Short-Form Certificate — for a partner or partners acting on behalf of a partnership:

State of Texas)

) ss.

County of)

This instrument was acknowledged before me on _____ (date) by _____ (name[s] of partner[s]) on behalf of _____ (name of partnership), a partnership.

_____ (Signature of Notary)   (Seal of Notary)

- Corporate Acknowledgment Short-Form Certificate — for a corporate officer acting on behalf of a corporation:

State of Texas)

) ss.

County of)

This instrument was acknowledged before me on _____ (date) by _____ (name of corporate officer), _____ (title of officer) of _____ (name of corporation acknowledging), a _____ (state of incorporation) corporation, on behalf of said corporation.

_____ (Signature of Notary)   (Seal of Notary)

- Representative Acknowledgment Short-Form Certificate — for a public officer, trustee, executor, administrator, guardian or other representative acting on behalf of an entity or person:

State of Texas)

) ss.

County of)

This instrument was acknowledged before me on _____ (date) by _____ (name of representative), _____ (title of representation) of _____ (name of entity or person represented).

_____ (Signature of Notary)   (Seal of Notary)

Texas law also allows modification of the preceding certificates as circumstances require. The authorization by law of particular certificate wordings does not prohibit the use of other appropriate wordings (TCPRC, Sec. 121.006).

Identification of Acknowledger. In executing an acknowledgment, the Notary must identify the signer through personal knowledge or another form of satisfactory evidence (TCPRC, Section 121.005). (See "Identifying Document Signers," *et seq.*, pages 41–45.)

Witnessing Signature not Required. For an acknowledgment, the document does not have to be signed in the Notary's presence. Rather, the document signer need only acknowledge having made the signature. As long as the signer appears before the Notary at the time of notarization to acknowledge having signed, the Notary may execute the acknowledgment. The document could have been signed an hour before, a week before, a year before, etc., as long as the signer appears before the Notary with the signed document at the time of notarization to admit that the signature is his or her own. However, for a jurat notarization, requiring an oath or affirmation, the document indeed must be signed in the presence of the Notary. (See "Jurats," pages 33–34.)

Terminology. In discussing the notarial act of acknowledgment, it is important to use the proper terminology. A Notary takes or executes an acknowledgment, while a document signer makes or gives an acknowledgment.

Who May Take Acknowledgments. Besides Notaries, a clerk of a district court or a judge or clerk of a county court can take acknowledgments and proofs within Texas (TCPRC, Sec. 121.001).

Outside of Texas, but inside the United States and its jurisdictions, acknowledgments and proofs of execution may be executed by the following (TCPRC, Sec. 121.001):

- Notaries of other U.S. states and jurisdictions.

- Clerks of courts of record having a seal.

- Commissioners of deeds appointed under the laws of Texas.

Outside of the United States and its jurisdictions, acknowledgments and proofs of execution may be executed by the following (TCPRC, Sec. 121.001):

- A Notary Public or other official authorized to administer oaths in the given jurisdiction.

- A minister, commissioner or charge d'affaires of the United States who is a resident of and is accredited in the given foreign country.

- A consul general, consul, vice-consul, commercial agent, vice-commercial agent, deputy consul or consular agent of the United States who is residing in the given foreign country.

A commissioned officer of the U.S. armed forces (or of a U.S. armed forces auxiliary) may take acknowledgments or proofs of execution from a member of the armed forces, a member of an armed forces auxiliary, or a member's spouse (TCPRC, Sec. 121.001). (See "Military-Officer Notarizations," pages 60–61.)

Certified Copies

Purpose. Texas Notaries have authority to certify that a copy of an original document is a complete and true reproduction of the document that was copied. The Notary's authority to certify copies is limited to documents which are not public records or recordable in the public record (TGC, Sec. 406.016).

Notaries may also certify copies of entries in their own official journals of notarial acts (TGC, Sec. 406.014). (See "Certified Copies of Notarial Records," pages 29–30.)

Procedure. The permanent custodian of the original document must present it to the Notary and request a certified copy. The Notary makes two photocopies — one for certification and one for the Notary's official records (NPEM).

A common request is to certify a copy of a college diploma, since only one such document exists and most people do not want to risk parting with the original when proof of their graduate status is requested by a prospective employer or school.

Precautions. Though a transcription or hand-rendered copy is not expressly prohibited, the NNA strongly recommends that Notaries only certify photocopies, to avert the high likelihood that something may be inadvertently omitted or incorrectly transcribed in a handmade copy. And, to minimize the opportunity for fraud, the making of the photocopy should be done by the Notary. Otherwise, the Notary should carefully compare the copy to the original, word for word, to ensure that it is complete and identical.

Copy Certification of Recordable Documents Prohibited. Texas Notaries are prohibited from certifying copies of recordable documents. A document does not have to be recorded, but merely recordable for the Notary to be prohibited from making a certified copy. In Texas, a passport is considered to be a recordable document and, therefore may not be certified (NPEM).

Vital Records. Texas Notaries are expressly prohibited from certifying copies of birth or death certificates, because these are recordable documents. Only officials in a bureau of vital statistics or other public record office may certify originals or copies of such certificates. (See "Bureaus of Vital Statistics," pages 129–132.) A Notary's "certification" of such a copy may lend credibility to what is actually a counterfeit or altered document (TGC, Sec. 406.016).

Additional Prohibited Documents. In addition to publicly recordable documents and vital records, the Secretary of State prohibits Texas Notaries from certifying copies of any of the following[1]:

- Passports

- Social Security cards

- Military ID

- Visas

- Certificates of naturalization

- Other ID cards/documents issued by the US Dept of Homeland Security

- Wills

- College or high school transcripts or diplomas

---

1 This information is available in the educational presentation provided on the Texas Secretary of State's Web site at http://www.sos.state.tx.us/statdoc/index.shtml.

Copies Certified by County Clerk. A county clerk may certify a copy of a notarial record or notarized document filed with that county clerk. A copy certified in this manner has the same authority as if it was certified by the Notary who kept the record or performed the notarization (TGC, Sec. 406.015).

Certificate for Certified Copy. The Secretary of State provides the following sample certificate wording for certifying a copy of a non-recordable document (NPEM):

State of Texas)

) ss.

County of)

On this _____ day of _____, _____, I certify that the preceding or attached document, and the duplicate retained by me as a notarial record, are true, exact, complete, and unaltered photocopies made by me of _____ (description of original document), presented to me by the document's custodian, _____ (name of original document's custodian), and that, to the best of my knowledge, the photocopied document is neither a public record nor a publicly recordable document, certified copies of which are available from an official source other than a Notary.

_____ (Signature of Notary)   (Seal of Notary)

Certified Copies of Notarial Records

Procedure. Members of the public may lawfully request Notary-certified photocopies of entries in the Notary's official journal or any notarial record in the Notary's office (TGC, Sec. 406.014).

Only photocopies — never hand-rendered duplications — of notarial records should be certified by a Notary. The notarial certificate should be attached to the front of the photocopy or copies, in contrast to loose acknowledgment certificates that usually are attached to a document's last page.

To prevent unauthorized viewing of notarial records, the careful Notary will only show and provide copies of entries or official papers in response to a written request that includes the signer(s) name(s), type of document, month, and year of notarization. In addition, the National Notary Association recommends that the individual requesting the notarial-record copy should be positively identified and sign in the Notary's record book.

Certificate for Certified Copy of Notarial Record. The Secretary
of State provides the following sample certificate wording for
certifying a copy of an entry or page from the Notary's journal or
other notarial record in the Notary's office (NPEM):

State of Texas   )

) ss.

County of   )

On this _____ day of _____, _____, I certify that the preceding or
attached document, and the duplicate retained by me as a notarial record, are
true, exact, complete and unaltered photocopies made by me of _____
(description of journal entry), held in my custody as a notarial record, and
that, to the best of my knowledge, the photocopied document is neither a
public record nor a publicly recordable document, certified copies of which
are available from an official source other than a Notary.

_____ (Signature of Notary)   (Seal of Notary)

Copy Certification by Document Custodian

Purpose. While not an official notarial act, copy certification
by document custodian may serve as an alternative to a
Notary-certified document copy when it would be inappropriate for
anyone but the document's permanent holder to certify the copy.

It should be noted that copy certification by document
custodian may not always be an acceptable substitute for a
Notary-certified copy, so the person requesting the act should
check to be sure it will serve the required purposes.

Notary Executes a Jurat. The permanent keeper of the
document — the document custodian — certifies the copy, not
the Notary. The document custodian makes a photocopy of the
original document; makes a written statement about the trueness,
correctness and completeness of the copy; signs that statement
before a Notary; and takes an oath or affirmation regarding the
truth of the statement. The Notary, having witnessed the signing
and given the oath or affirmation, executes a jurat.

Certificate for Copy Certification by Document Custodian. Copy
certification by document custodian is, for the Notary's purposes,
simply a jurat. The custodian's statement is not prescribed by
law. The National Notary Association recommends the following
wording, including the jurat:

State of Texas   )

) ss.

County of   )

I, _____ (name of custodian of original document), hereby swear (or affirm) that the attached reproduction of _____ (description of original document) is a true, correct, and complete photocopy of a document in my possession.

_____ (signature of custodian) _____ (address)

Subscribed and sworn to (or affirmed) before me this _____ day of _____, _____, by _____ (name of custodian).

_____ (Signature of Notary)   (Seal of Notary)

Depositions and Affidavits

Purpose. A deposition is a signed transcript of the signer's oral statements taken down for use in a judicial proceeding. The deposition signer is called the deponent.

An affidavit is a signed statement made under oath or affirmation by a person called an affiant, and it is used for a variety of purposes both in and out of court.

For both a deposition and an affidavit, the Notary must administer an oath or affirmation and complete some form of jurat, which the Notary signs and seals.

Depositions. With a deposition, both sides in a lawsuit or court case have the opportunity to question the deponent. The questions and answers are transcribed into a written statement, then signed and sworn to before an oath-administering official.

Texas Notaries have the power to take depositions — meaning, to transcribe the words spoken aloud by a deponent — but this duty is most often executed by trained and certified shorthand reporters, also known as court reporters (TGC, Sec. 406.016).

Affidavits. Affidavits are used in and out of court for a variety of purposes, from declaring losses to an insurance company to declaring U.S. citizenship before traveling to a foreign country. An affidavit is a document containing a statement voluntarily signed and sworn to (or affirmed) before a Notary or other oath-administering official. If used in a judicial proceeding, only one side in the case need participate in the affidavit process, in contrast to the deposition.

In an affidavit, the Notary's certificate typically sandwiches the affiant's signed statement, with the venue and affiant's name at the top of the document and the jurat wording at the end. The Notary is responsible for the venue, affiant's name, and any notarial text at the beginning and end of the affidavit, and the affiant is responsible for the signed statement in the middle.

Certificate for Depositions. The Secretary of State provides the following sample certificate wording for depositions (NPEM):

- Certificate for deposition in response to written questions:

The State of Texas   )

County of _____   )

_____ (Plaintiff)   ) In the _____Court

v.   ) of _____ County, Texas

_____ (Defendant)   ) Cause No. _____

I hereby certify that the foregoing answers of _____, the witness forenamed, were signed and sworn to before me on _____ (date), by said witness.

_____ (Signature of Notary)   (Seal of Notary)

- Certificate for deposition in response to oral questions:

The State of Texas   )

County of _____   )

_____ (Plaintiff)   ) In the _____Court

v.   ) of _____ County, Texas

_____ (Defendant)   ) Cause No. _____

I, _____ (Notary Public's name), Notary Public in _____ County, Texas, do hereby certify that the said witness _____ (name) was first sworn to testify the truth and nothing but the truth; that he/she was then carefully examined; that his/her testimony which is above given was by me reduced to writing (or typewriting) (or to writing or typewriting by _____ (name), a person under my personal supervision; or by the deponent himself/herself in my presence) and by no other person, and that after it had been so reduced to writing (or typewriting) subscribed by the deponent before me all on _____ day of _____, _____ (year).

_____ (Signature of Notary)   (Seal of Notary)

Certificate for Affidavits. Affidavits require jurat certificates. (See "Jurats," below.)

Oath (Affirmation) for Depositions and Affidavits. If no other wording is prescribed, a Notary may use the following language in administering an oath (affirmation) for an affidavit or deposition:

Do you solemnly swear that the statements made in this affidavit (or deposition) are the truth, the whole truth, and nothing but the truth, so help you God?

(Do you solemnly affirm that the statements made in this affidavit [or deposition] are the truth, the whole truth, and nothing but the truth?)

For both oath and affirmation, the affiant must respond aloud and affirmatively, with, "I do," or, "Yes," or the like.

Jurats

Part of Verification. In notarizing affidavits, depositions and other forms of written verification requiring an oath by the signer, the Notary typically executes a jurat.

Purpose. While the purpose of an acknowledgment is to positively identify a document signer, the purpose of a verification with jurat is to compel truthfulness by appealing to the signer's conscience and fear of criminal penalties for perjury.

In executing a jurat, a Notary certifies the following:

- The signer personally appeared before the Notary at the time of notarization on the date and in the county indicated (notarization based on a telephone call or on familiarity with a signature is not acceptable)

- The Notary watched the signature being made at the time of notarization

- The Notary administered an oath or affirmation to the signer

Certificate for a Jurat. A typical jurat is the wording,
"Subscribed and sworn to (or affirmed) before me on this _____
(date) by _____ (name of signer)..." or similar language.
"Subscribed" means "signed." The Secretary of State provides the
following jurat wording (NPEM):

State of Texas   )
) ss.
County of   )

Sworn to and subscribed before me the _____ day of _____,
_____ (year).

_____ (Signature of Notary)   (Seal of Notary)

Identification. When executing a jurat, the prudent Notary will
positively identify each signer, even though identification is not
required by law for a jurat as it is for an acknowledgment.

Wording for Jurat Oath (Affirmation). If not otherwise
prescribed by law, a Texas Notary may use the following
or similar wording to administer an oath (or affirmation) in
conjunction with a jurat:

Do you solemnly swear that the statements in this document are true to the
best of your knowledge and belief, so help you God?

(Do you solemnly affirm that the statements in this document are true to the
best of your knowledge and belief?)

Oaths and Affirmations

Purpose. An oath is a solemn, spoken pledge to a Supreme
Being. An affirmation is a solemn, spoken pledge on one's own
personal honor, with no reference to a Supreme Being. Both are
usually a promise or pledge of truthfulness or fidelity and have
the same legal effect. In taking an oath or affirmation in an official
proceeding, a person may be subject to criminal penalties for
perjury should he or she fail to be truthful.

An oath or affirmation can be a full-fledged notarial act in its
own right, as when giving an oath of office to a public official
(when "swearing in" a public official), or it can be part of the

process of notarizing a document (e.g., executing a jurat or swearing in a credible identifying witness).

A person who objects to taking an oath — pledging to a Supreme Being — may instead be given an affirmation, which does not refer to a Supreme Being.

Power to Administer. Texas Notaries are authorized to administer oaths and affirmations (TGC, Sec. 406.016).

Wording for Oath (Affirmation). If law does not dictate otherwise, a Texas Notary may use the following or similar words in administering an oath (or affirmation):

- Oath (affirmation) for an affiant signing an affidavit or a deponent signing a deposition:

Do you solemnly swear that the statements in this document are true to the best of your knowledge and belief, so help you God?

(Do you solemnly affirm that the statements in this document are true to the best of your knowledge and belief?)

- Oath (affirmation) for a credible identifying witness identifying a document signer who is in the Notary's presence:

Do you solemnly swear that you personally know this signer truly holds the identity he (or she) claims, so help you God?

(Do you solemnly affirm that you personally know this signer truly holds the identity he [or she] claims?)

- Oath (affirmation) for a subscribing witness identifying a document signer who is not in the Notary's presence:

Do you solemnly swear that you saw (name of the document signer) sign his/her name to this document or that he/she acknowledged to you having executed it for the purposes and consideration therein stated, and that you signed the document at the request of (name of the document signer), so help you God?

(Do you solemnly affirm that you saw [name of the document signer] sign his/her name to this document or that he/she acknowledged to you having executed it for the purposes and consideration therein stated, and that you signed the document at the request of [name of the document signer]?)

The oath or affirmation wording must be spoken aloud, and the person taking the oath or affirmation must answer affirmatively with "I do," "Yes," or the like. A nod or grunt is not a clear and sufficient response. If a person is mute and unable to speak, the Notary may rely on written notes to communicate.

Ceremony and Gestures. To impress upon the oath-taker or affirmant the importance of truthfulness, the Notary is encouraged to lend a sense of ceremony and formality to the oath or affirmation. During administration of an oath or affirmation, the Notary and document signer traditionally raise their right hands, though this is not a legal requirement. Notaries generally have discretion to use words and gestures they feel will most compellingly appeal to the conscience of the oath-taker or affirmant.

Proof of Acknowledgment by Handwriting

Purpose. In very limited situations, a proof of acknowledgment by handwriting may be taken. To do so, two witnesses, who are well acquainted with the handwriting of an unavailable principal signer, must personally appear and swear by deposition or affidavit that the signature of the principal signer is genuine (TCPRC, Sec. 121.011).

In addition, the signature of at least one witness who signed the document must also be similarly proved. If the principal signer signed by mark, then the signatures of at least two witnesses to the mark must be similarly proved (TCPRC, Sec. 121.011).

Requirements for Use. The execution of a document may be proved by handwriting only if one of the following is true (TCPRC, Sec. 121.011):

- The document signer and all of the witnesses are dead.

- The signer and all of the witnesses are not Texas residents.

- The residences of the signer and all of the witnesses are unknown to the person seeking to prove execution of the document and cannot be ascertained.

- The witnesses have become legally incompetent to testify.

- The signer refuses to acknowledge the execution of the document and all of the witnesses are deceased, not residents of Texas, legally incompetent, or their places of residence are unknown.

In Lieu of Acknowledgment. On recordable documents, a proof of acknowledgment by handwriting is regarded as an acceptable substitute for an acknowledgment (TCPRC, Sec. 121.011).

Witnesses. Two disinterested witnesses are required to establish proof of a signature. These witnesses must personally know the signer, must be well acquainted with the signer's handwriting, and must be able to recognize the signature as genuine (TCPRC, Secs. 121.011).

Depositions or Affidavits Required. The witnesses to a proof of acknowledgment by handwriting must give evidence in the form of a deposition or affidavit which must satisfactorily prove to the Notary each requirement — that they are disinterested witnesses, that they personally know the signer, that they are well acquainted with the signer's handwriting, and that they determine the signature to be genuine.

The Notary must certify the witnesses' testimony and attach a certificate with the Notary's official seal, along with the depositions or affidavits of the witnesses to the document (TCPRC, Sec. 121.011).

Certificate for Proof of Acknowledgment by Handwriting. A sample certificate for proof of acknowledgment by handwriting is not prescribed by law. Since such acts are extremely rare and complex, the National Notary Association recommends that Notaries perform proofs of acknowledgment by handwriting only under the supervision of an attorney who would prepare the required certificates.

Oath (Affirmation) for Handwriting Witness. An acceptable oath for the witness might be:

Do you solemnly swear that you personally know (name of signer), that you are well acquainted with (name of signer)'s handwriting, that you determine the signature on (description of document) to be that of (name of signer), and that you have no personal beneficial or financial interest in the document, so help you God?

(Do you solemnly affirm that you personally know [name of signer], that you are well acquainted with [name of signer]'s handwriting, that you determine the signature on [description of document] to be that of [name of signer], and that you have no personal beneficial or financial interest in the document?)

Subpoena of Witness. Notaries may issue a subpoena — though this power is rarely used — to require the appearance of a witness to a document to testify about its execution (TCPRC, Secs. 121.003 and 121.013). (See "Subpoena of Witness," page 40.)

Proof of Acknowledgment by Subscribing Witness

Purpose. In executing a proof of acknowledgment by subscribing witness (also called a proof of execution by a subscribing witness), a Notary certifies that the signature of a person who does not appear before the Notary — the principal signer — is genuine and freely made based on the sworn testimony of another person who does appear — a subscribing (signing) witness.

Proofs of acknowledgment by a subscribing witness are used when the principal signer is out of town or otherwise unavailable to appear before a Notary. Proofs should never be used because the principal signer prefers not to take the time to personally appear before a Notary. Because of the high potential for fraud when executing proofs, they should be used only when there is no other option.

In Lieu of Acknowledgment. On recordable documents, a proof of acknowledgment by subscribing witness is regarded as an acceptable substitute for an acknowledgment (TCPRC, Sec. 121.009).

Subscribing Witness. A subscribing witness is a person who watches a principal sign a document (or who personally takes the principal's acknowledgment) and then subscribes (signs) his or her own name on the document at the principal's request. This witness brings that document to a Notary on the principal's behalf and takes an oath or affirmation from the Notary to the effect that the principal did indeed willingly sign (or acknowledge signing) the document and request the witness to also sign the document (TCPRC, Sec. 121.009).

The ideal subscribing witness personally knows the principal signer and has no personal beneficial or financial interest in the document or transaction. It would be foolish of the Notary, for example, to rely on the word of a subscribing witness presenting for notarization a power of attorney that names this very witness as attorney in fact.

<u>Identifying Subscribing Witness</u>. The subscribing witness must be personally known to the Notary or the identity must be proved on the oath of a credible identifying witness who is personally known to the Notary (TCPRC, Sec. 121.009).

<u>Certificate for Proof of Acknowledgment by Subscribing Witness</u>. Texas law specifies the following certificate (sometimes called a "witness jurat") or substantially similar wording for a proof of acknowledgment by a subscribing witness (TCPRC, Sec. 121.010):

State of Texas　　）
　　　　　　　　　）ss.
County of　　　　）

Before me _____ (name and title of officer), on this day personally appeared _____ (name of subscribing witness), known to me (or proved to me on the oath of _____ [name of credible identifying witness]) to be the person whose name is subscribed as a witness to the foregoing instrument of writing, and, after being duly sworn by me, stated on oath that he/she saw _____ (name of principal signer), the grantor or person who executed the foregoing instrument, subscribe the same (or that the grantor or person who executed such instrument of writing acknowledged in his/her presence that he/she had executed the same for the purposes and consideration therein expressed), and that he/she had signed the same as a witness at the request of the grantor (or person who executed the same).

Given under my hand and seal of office this _____ day of _____, _____ A.D.

_____ (Signature of Notary)　(Seal of Notary)

<u>Oath (Affirmation) for Subscribing Witness</u>. An acceptable oath for the subscribing witness might be:

Do you solemnly swear that you saw (name of the document signer) sign his/her name to this document or that he/she acknowledged to you having executed it for the purposes and consideration therein stated, and that you signed the document at the request of (name of the document signer), so help you God?

(Do you solemnly affirm that you saw [name of the document signer] sign his/her name to this document or that he/she acknowledged to you having executed it for the purposes and consideration therein stated, and that you signed the document at the request of [name of the document signer]?)

Journal. It is recommended that the subscribing witness then sign the Notary's journal.

Interpreters. In a proceeding to prove the execution of a document, Notaries have the authority to employ and swear interpreters. A Notary may not personally serve as an interpreter in a translation in which the Notary would have to administer an oath to the interpreter (TCPRC, Sec. 121.003).

Subpoena of Witness. Though this power is rarely used, Texas Notaries may issue a subpoena to require the appearance of a witness to a document to testify about its execution. The person who wants the document proven must submit a sworn application stating that a witness refuses to appear and testify about the document's execution and that the document cannot be proven without the witness's testimony. A witness may not be required to leave his or her county of residence, but if temporarily in the county where the proof is sought, the witness may then be required to appear (TCPRC, Secs. 121.003 and 121.013).

Protests

Purpose. In rare instances, Texas Notaries may be asked to protest a negotiable instrument for nonpayment. A protest is a written statement by a Notary or other authorized officer verifying that payment was not received on an instrument such as a bank draft. Failure to pay is called dishonor. Before issuing a certificate of protest, the Notary must present the bank draft or other instrument to the person, firm or institution obliged to pay, a procedure called presentment (TGC, Sec. 406.016).

Antiquated Act. In the 19th century, protests were common notarial acts in the United States, but they rarely are performed today due to the advent of modern electronic communications and resulting changes in our banking and financial systems. Modern Notaries most often encounter protests in the context of international commerce.

Special Knowledge Required. Notarial acts of protest are complicated and varied, requiring a special knowledge of financial and legal terminology. Only Notaries who have the requisite special knowledge, or who are acting under the supervision of an experienced bank officer or an attorney familiar with the Uniform Commercial Code, should attempt a protest.

Certificate for Protest. The Secretary of State provides the following certificate wording for a protest (NPEM):

(Insert bill or note or copy thereof)

United States of America   )

State of Texas   ) ss.

County of _____   )

Be it known that on the _____ day of _____, _____ (year), at the request of _____ (name of person appearing before Notary), of _____ (name of person or entity represented), I _____ (name of Notary), a Notary Public duly commissioned and sworn, residing in _____ County, Texas, did present the original _____ (description of instrument) hereto attached for $_____, with accrued interest thereon of $_____, dated _____, _____ (year), and demanded payment (or acceptance) thereof which was refused.

Whereupon I, at the request of the aforesaid _____ (name of person appearing before Notary), did protest and by these presents do protest, as well against the drawer, maker, endorsers, and acceptors of said instruments as against all others, whom it may concern, for exchange, costs, charges, damages, and interest already incurred and hereinafter to be incurred by reason of non-payment thereof. I further certify that on _____, _____, notice in writing of the foregoing presentment, demand, refusal, and protest was given by _____ (persons and status) by depositing notices thereof in the post office at _____, Texas, postage paid, directed as follows: _____. I further certify that notices were left as follows:

Notice left for _____ (name) at _____ (address)

Notice left for _____ (name) at _____ (address)

(Each of the named places the reputed place of residence of the person for whom the notice was left.)

In testimony whereof I have hereunto set my hand and affixed my seal of office at _____ (county), Texas, on _____ day of _____, _____ (year).

_____ (Signature of Notary)   (Seal of Notary)

PRACTICES AND PROCEDURES

Identifying Document Signers

Acknowledgments. In taking acknowledgments for any document, Texas law requires the Notary to identify the acknowledger. The following three methods of identification are acceptable, any one of which is considered satisfactory evidence of identity (TCPRC, Sec. 121.005):

- The Notary's personal knowledge of the signer's identity (See "Personal Knowledge of Identity," below.)

- The oath or affirmation of a personally known credible identifying witness (See "Credible Identifying Witnesses," pages 43–44.)

- Reliable, current identification documents or ID cards (See "Identification Documents," pages 44–46.)

Identification for Other Notarial Acts. While the law specifies identification standards only for acknowledgers, the prudent and conscientious Notary will apply those same standards in identifying any signer, whether for an acknowledgment or a jurat.

Capacity. Texas law is not clear on whether Notaries are required to verify the capacity in which a person signs. However, the law does state that for an acknowledgment by a person acting in a representative capacity — such as corporate officer, trustee, partner to a partnership, attorney in fact or other capacity — the signer must personally appear before the Notary and acknowledge executing the instrument by proper authority in the capacity claimed for the purposes stated in the document (TCPRC, Sec. 121.006).

Personal Knowledge of Identity

Definition. The safest and most reliable method of identifying a document signer is for the Notary to depend on his or her own personal knowledge of the signer's identity. Personal knowledge means familiarity with an individual resulting from interactions with that person over a sufficient period of time to eliminate every reasonable doubt that the person has the identity claimed.

Texas law does not specify how long a Notary must be acquainted with an individual before personal knowledge of identity may be claimed. The Notary's common sense must prevail. In general, the longer the Notary is acquainted with a person, and the more random interactions the Notary has had with that person, the more likely the individual is indeed personally known.

For instance, the Notary might safely regard a friend since childhood as personally known, but would be foolish to consider a person met for the first time the previous day as such. Whenever the Notary has a reasonable doubt about a signer's identity, that individual should not be considered personally known, and the identification should be made through either a credible identifying witness or reliable identification documents (TCPRC, Sec. 121.005).

Credible Identifying Witnesses

Purpose. When a document signer is not personally known to the Notary and is not able to present reliable ID cards, that signer may be identified on the oath (or affirmation) of a credible identifying witness.

Qualifications. A credible identifying witness must be personally known to the Notary and the document signer must be personally known to the credible identifying witness. (See "Personal Knowledge of Identity," preceding.) There should be a chain of personal knowledge linking the Notary to the credible identifying witness to the signer. In a sense, a credible identifying witness is a walking, talking ID card (TCPRC, Sec. 121.005).

A reliable credible identifying witness should have a reputation for honesty. The witness should be a reasonably intelligent individual who would not be tricked, cajoled, bullied or otherwise influenced into identifying someone he or she does not really know. The witness, ideally, should have no personal beneficial or financial interest in the transaction requiring a notarial act.

Oath (Affirmation) for Credible Identifying Witness. An oath or affirmation must be administered to the credible identifying witness by the Notary to compel truthfulness.

If not otherwise prescribed by law, a Texas Notary may use the following or similar wording to administer an oath (or affirmation) to credible identifying witnesses:

Do you solemnly swear that you know the signer truly holds the identity he (or she) claims?

(Do you solemnly affirm that you know the signer truly holds the identity he [or she] claims?)

Journal Entry. Each credible identifying witness's name and residence address must be recorded in the Notary's journal. Prudent Notaries also will ask witnesses to sign the journal (TGC, Sec. 406.014).

Not a Subscribing Witness. Do not confuse a credible identifying witness with a subscribing witness. A credible identifying witness vouches for the identity of a signer who appears before the Notary. A subscribing witness vouches for the genuineness of the signature of a signer who does not appear before the Notary. (See "Proof of Acknowledgment by Subscribing Witness," pages 38–40.)

Identification Documents (ID Cards)

Acceptable Identification Documents. Texas requires an identifying document or card relied on by a Notary to identify a stranger must be current and issued by a federal or state governmental agency and must contain a photograph and signature of the bearer (TCPRC, Sec. 121.005 and NPEM).

Among the IDs authorized for use by Texas Notaries are state driver's and official nondriver's IDs, U.S. passports, U.S. military IDs and resident alien IDs or "green cards" issued by the U.S. Citizenship and Immigration Services.

The National Notary Association urges Notaries to rely only on IDs with a photograph, a physical description (e.g., "brown hair, green eyes"), and a signature of the bearer. Most government-issued IDs contain all three components.

Identification Documents for Real Estate Transactions. Effective September 1, 2011, in addition to the acceptable forms of written identification listed above, for the purposes of a deed or other instrument relating to a residential real estate transaction, a person's identity may be proved by a current passport issued by a foreign country (TCPRC Sec. 121.0005 [a][3]). In addition to conveyance deeds, documents for which a foreign passport may be accepted may include deeds of trust, various affidavits supporting refinance or purchase transactions and powers of attorney for the purpose of conveying real property or executing documents related to real estate loan transactions.

Unacceptable Identification Documents. Social Security cards, birth certificates and credit cards are worthless as identifying documents.

Multiple Identification. While one identification document is sufficient to identify a signer, the Notary may ask for more.

Fraudulent Identification. Identification documents are the least secure of the three methods of identification, because phony ID cards are common. The Notary should scrutinize each card for evidence of counterfeiting, or for evidence that it is a genuine card issued to an impostor.

Some clues that an ID card may have been tampered with include: mismatched type styles, a photograph raised from the surface, a signature that does not match the signature on the document, and smudges, erasures, smears, or discolorations.

Possible tip-offs to a counterfeit ID card include: misspelled words, a brand new-looking card with an old date of issuance or two cards with exactly the same photograph.

Some possible indications that a card may have been issued to an impostor include: the card's birth date or address are unknown to the bearer, all the ID cards seem brand new.

Journal of Notarial Acts

Requirement. Texas Notaries are required to make a record in a Notary journal of every document notarized (TGC, Sec. 406.014 and TCPRC, Sec. 121.012).

Court Clerk Exemption. A court clerk, notarizing documents for the court, is not required to keep a journal (TGC, Sec. 406.014).

Journal Format. The Texas Government Code states that Notaries must keep records in a "book," while the Civil Practices and Remedies Code indicates that records of acknowledgments and proofs must be recorded in a "well-bound book" (G.C. Sec. 406.014[a] and TCPRC Sec. 121.012[a]). The best Notary journals are permanently bound books (not loose-leaf) with preprinted page numbers.

Texas Notaries may record journal entries electronically in a computer or other storage device (T.G.C. Sec. 406.014[e]). For example, a Notary may record journal entries in a computer spreadsheet, database or other program designed specifically to be used as a Notary journal as long as the required entries are recorded. (See "Journal Entries," below).

Journal Entries. For each notarization, the journal must contain the following entries (TGC, Sec. 406.014):

- The date of each document notarized.

- The date on which the notarization was performed.

- The name of the signer, grantor or maker.

- The signer's, grantor's or maker's residence address.

- A statement of how the signer, grantor or maker was identified.

    — If by personal knowledge or credible identifying witness, the words, "Personal Knowledge" or "Credible Identifying Witness."

    — If by an ID card, the type of ID, its issuing agency and date of issuance or expiration. A Notary Public other than a court appointed clerk notarizing court documents is prohibited from recording the identification card number (TAC, Sec. 87.60).

- In the case of a proof, the residence address of the witness and whether the witness was personally known or introduced by a credible identifying witness.

    — If introduced by a credible identifying witness, also include the credible identifying witness's name and residence address.

- The name and residence address of the grantee (the recipient of the property), if applicable.

- If land is conveyed or charged, the name and residence address of the original grantee and the county where the land is located.

- A brief description of the document (the title or type of the document or proceeding — e.g., grant deed, affidavit of support, oath of office, etc.).

Entry for Fees. Notaries must keep a fee book — a record of the fees charged for notarial services — which shall be subject to public inspection at any time. This fee book may be the same book as the Notary journal, with the fees charged included with other journal entries (TGC, Sec. 603.006 and NPEM).

Additional Entries. Notaries may include additional information in their journals that is pertinent to a given notarization. Many Notaries, for example, ask for a signature in the Notary journal as proof the signer personally appeared and as a deterrent to fraud. And many also enter the telephone numbers of signers and witnesses as well as the address where the notarization was performed, if not at the Notary's office. A description of the document signer's demeanor (e.g., "The signer appeared very nervous") or notations about the identity of other persons who were present for the notarization may also be pertinent.

One important entry to include is the signer's representative capacity — attorney in fact, trustee, guardian, corporate officer or other capacity — if not signing on his or her own behalf.

Effective September 1, 2009, Texas Notaries may no longer record a signer's thumbprint in their Notary journal (House Bill 3186, 2009).

Inspection of Notarial Records. Since the Notary's official journal is kept for the public benefit, members of the public may lawfully request to examine it (TGC, Sec. 406.014).

The careful Notary only will show and provide copies of entries in response to a written request that includes the signer(s) name(s), type of document, and the month and year of notarization. In addition, the National Notary Association recommends that the individual requesting the notarial-record copy should be positively identified and sign in the Notary's record book.

Although the journal may be inspected, the Notary never should be relaxed about its security. Any inspection must be performed in the Notary's presence. No one should be allowed to take possession of the journal, even for just a few minutes.

Copy of Journal Entry. Notaries are permitted to certify copies of entries in their own official journals or any record in their office and to charge 50 cents for each page certified in addition to the $6 fee for the certificate (TGC, Sec. 406.014 and 406.024).

The Secretary of State provides the following sample certificate wording for certifying a copy of an entry or page from the Notary's journal or other record in the Notary's office (NPEM):

State of Texas   )

) ss.

County of   )

On this _____ day of _____, _____, I certify that the preceding or attached document, and the duplicate retained by me as a notarial record, are true, exact, complete, and unaltered photocopies made by me of _____ (description of journal entry), held in my custody as a notarial record, and that, to the best of my knowledge, the photocopied document is neither a public record nor a publicly recordable document, certified copies of which are available from an official source other than a Notary.

_____ (Signature of Notary)   (Seal of Notary)

<u>Never Surrender Journal</u>. Notaries never should surrender control of their official journals to anyone, unless expressly subpoenaed by a court order. Even when an employer has paid for the Notary's official journal and seal, they go with the Notary upon termination of employment; no person but the Notary can lawfully possess and use these official adjuncts of office.

<u>Disposition of Notary Records</u>. Upon resignation, death or removal from the office, the Notary, or his or her representative, must deposit the Notary's journal with the clerk of the county where the Notary resides or resided (TGC, Sec. 406.022).

<u>Electronic Journal Permitted</u>. Texas Notaries are permitted to record notarial acts electronically in a computer or other storage device (TGC, Sec. 406.014).

Notarial Certificate

<u>Requirement</u>. In notarizing any document, a Notary must complete a notarial certificate. The certificate is wording that indicates exactly what the Notary has certified. The notarial certificate may be typed or printed on the document itself or on an attachment to it. The certificate should contain the following:

- A venue indicating where the notarization is being performed. "State of Texas, County of _____," is the typical venue wording, with the appropriate county inserted in the blank. The letters "SS" or "SCT." sometimes appear after the venue; they abbreviate the Latin word *scilicet*, meaning "in particular" or "namely."

- A statement of particulars which indicates what the notarization has certified. An acknowledgment certificate would include such wording as: "This instrument was acknowledged before me on _____ (date) by _____ (name of signer)." A jurat certificate would include such wording as: "Signed and sworn to (or affirmed) before me on _____ (date) by _____ (name of signer)."

- A testimonium clause, which may be optional if the date is included in the statement of particulars: "Witness my hand and official seal, this _____ day of _____, _____." In this phrase, the Notary formally attests to the truthfulness of the preceding facts in the certificate. "Hand" means signature.

- The official signature of the Notary, exactly as the name appears on the commission certificate and on the Notary's official seal.

- The official seal of the Notary. On many certificates, the letters "L.S." appear, indicating where the Notary's seal is to be placed. These letters abbreviate the Latin term *locus sigilli*, meaning "place of the seal." An inking seal should be placed near but not over the letters, so that wording imprinted by the seal or stamp will not be obscured. An embossing seal may be placed directly over the letters — slightly displacing portions of the characters and leaving a clue that document examiners can use to distinguish an original from a counterfeit photocopy.

Loose Certificates. When appropriate certificate wording is not preprinted on the document for the Notary to fill out, a loose certificate may be attached. Normally, this form is stapled to the document's left margin on the signature page. Only one side of the certificate should be stapled, so it can be lifted to view the document beneath it.

To prevent a loose certificate from being removed and fraudulently placed on another document, there are precautions a Notary can take. For instance, the Notary can write a brief description of the document on the certificate: e.g., "This certificate is attached to a _____ (title or type of document),

dated _____, of _____ (number) pages, also signed by
_____ (name[s] of other signer[s])."

While fraud-deterrent steps such as this one can make it
much more difficult for a loose certificate to be removed and
misused, there is no absolute protection against removal and
misuse. Notaries, however, absolutely must ensure that while
a certificate remains in their control, it is attached only to its
intended document. A Notary never must give or mail a signed
and stamped notarial certificate to another person and trust that
person to attach it to a particular document; this would be an
indefensible action in a civil court of law.

Do Not Pre-Sign/Seal Certificates. A Notary should never sign
or seal certificates ahead of time or permit other persons to attach
loose notarial certificates to documents. Nor should the Notary
send an unattached, signed and sealed, loose certificate through
the mail, even if requested to do so by a signer who previously
appeared before the Notary. These actions may facilitate fraud or
forgery, and they could subject the Notary to lawsuits to recover
damages resulting from the Notary's neglect or misconduct.

Notary Seal

Requirement. A Texas Notary must affix an impression of an
official seal on the certificate portion of every document notarized
(TGC, Sec. 406.013).

Format. The seal may either be circular, not more than two
inches in diameter, or rectangular, not more than one inch in
height and two and one-half inches in length. The seal must have
a serrated or milled-edge border (TGC, Sec. 406.013).

Stamp or Embosser. The seal must print in ink or emboss a
photographically reproducible impression. A hand-drawn seal is not
acceptable. A notarized document sent electronically must legibly
reproduce the required elements of the seal (TGC, Sec. 406.013).

Because the image must be photocopiable, most Notaries use
an inked rubber stamp seal, since an embossment needs to be
smudged or darkened in order to be photocopiable. An embosser
may be used in addition to the required photographically
reproducible seal, but it must not be used over this seal or over
the Notary's signature.

<u>Required Information</u>. The Notary seal must contain the following elements (TGC, Sec. 406.013):

- Name of the Notary

- The words "Notary Public, State of Texas" around a star of five points

- The Notary's commission expiration date

<u>L.S.</u> The letters "L.S." — abbreviating the Latin term *locus sigilli*, meaning "location of the seal" — appear on many notarial certificates to indicate where the Notary seal should be placed. While an embossing seal may be affixed over these letters, an inking stamp should be imprinted near but not over the letters.

<u>Placement of the Seal Impression</u>. The Notary's official seal impression should be placed near the Notary's signature.

Whenever possible — and especially with documents that will be submitted to a public recorder — the Notary should avoid affixing the seal over any text on the document or certificate. Some recorders will reject documents if writing or document text intrudes within the borders of the Notary's seal. If there is no room for a seal, the Notary may have no choice but to complete and attach a loose certificate that duplicates the notarial wording on the document. With documents that will not be publicly recorded, however, the recipient may allow the Notary to affix the seal over boilerplate text — a document's standard clauses or sections.

Fees for Notarial Services

<u>Maximum Fees</u>. The following maximum fees for performing notarial acts are allowed by Texas law (TGC, Sec. 406.024):

- <u>Acknowledgments — $6</u>. For taking an acknowledgment, the Notary may charge $6 for the first signature on a document, plus $1 for each additional signature on that same document.

- <u>Certified Copies — $6</u>. For certifying a copy, the Notary may charge $6 for each certified copy certificate.

- <u>Certified Copies of Notarial Records — 50 cents</u>. For providing a copy of a Notary record — either an entry in the

Notary's official journal or any paper in the Notary's office — the Notary may charge 50 cents for each page in addition to the $6 fee for the certificate.

- Depositions — $6 plus 50 cents per 100 words. For swearing a witness to a deposition, including completing the certificate, affixing the seal and other connected business, the fee is $6. For taking the deposition of a witness, the fee is 50 cents for each 100 words.

- Jurats — $6. For executing a jurat on an affidavit or other form of verification upon oath or affirmation, the Notary may charge $6 for each signature.

- Oaths and Affirmations — $6. For administering an oath or affirmation with certificate and seal, the Notary may charge $6.

- Proof of Acknowledgment — $6. For taking a proof of acknowledgment, the Notary may charge $6 for the first signature of each absent principal signer, plus $1 for each additional signature proven.

- Protests — $4. For protesting a bill or note, the fee is $4. For serving a notice of protest, the fee is $1. For protesting in all other cases, the fee is $4. For the certificate and seal to a protest, the fee is $4.

- All Other Notarial Acts — $6. For performing any other notarial act or for completing a certificate and seal not otherwise provided for, the Notary may charge $6.

Travel Fees. Charges for travel by a Notary are not specified by law. Such fees are proper only if Notary and signer agree beforehand on the amount to be charged. The signer must understand a travel fee is not stipulated in law and is separate from the notarial fees described above.

Option Not to Charge. Notaries are not required to charge for their notarial services. They also may charge any fee less than the statutory maximum.

Overcharging. If a Notary charges more than the legally prescribed fees, the Notary is liable to the person overcharged for four times the fee unlawfully demanded (TGC, Secs. 406.024 and 603.010).

In addition, if a Notary charges more than the statutory maximum, his or her commission may be suspended or revoked by the Secretary of State (TGC, Sec. 406.009).

Fee Book. Notaries must keep a fee book — a record of the fees charged for notarial services — which shall be subject to public inspection at any time. This fee book may be the same as the Notary journal, with the fees charged included with other journal entries (TGC, Sec. 603.006). (See "Journal of Notarial Acts," pages 45–48.)

Posting of Fees. A Texas Notary is required to post in some conspicuous place in his or her office a table of the fees allowed by law to be charged (TGC, Sec. 603.008).

Obligation to Itemize. A Notary must itemize or be prepared to itemize in a signed bill the fees he or she charges for services (TGC, Sec. 603.007).

Disqualifying Interest

Impartiality. Notaries are appointed by the state to be impartial, disinterested witnesses whose screening duties help ensure the integrity of important legal and commercial transactions. Lack of impartiality by a Notary throws doubt on the integrity and lawfulness of any transaction. A Notary may never notarize his or her own signature, or notarize in a transaction in which the Notary has a financial or beneficial interest.

Financial or Beneficial Interest. A Notary should not perform any notarization related to a transaction in which that Notary or the Notary's spouse has a direct financial or beneficial interest. A financial or beneficial interest exists when the Notary or the Notary's spouse is individually named as a principal in a financial transaction or when the Notary receives an advantage, right, privilege, property or fee valued in excess of the lawfully prescribed notarial fee.

In regard to real estate transactions, a Notary generally is considered to have a disqualifying financial or beneficial interest when that Notary or the Notary's spouse is a grantor or grantee, a mortgagor or mortgagee, a trustor or trustee, a vendor or vendee, a lessor or lessee or a beneficiary in any way of the transaction.

Employees, Officers and Shareholders. An employee of a corporation may notarize documents in which the corporation has an interest. Also, an officer who is a shareholder in a corporation may notarize documents in which the corporation has an interest — unless the corporation has 1,000 or fewer shareholders and the officer owns more than one-tenth of one percent of the issued and outstanding stock (TCPRC, Sec. 121.002).

Relatives. State officials strongly discourage Notaries from notarizing for persons related by blood or marriage, because of the likelihood of a financial or beneficial interest, whether large or small. This is especially pertinent with spouses, because Texas is a state with community property laws (NPEM).

Refusal of Services

Legal Request for Services. Notaries must honor all lawful and reasonable requests to notarize, whether or not the person requesting the act is a client or customer of the Notary or the Notary's employer (TCPRC, Sec. 121.014).

Notaries are appointed by the state of Texas to serve the general public, even when their appointment fee, seal and notarial supplies are paid for by a private employer.

A person's race, gender, religion, nationality, ethnicity, lifestyle or politics is never legitimate cause for refusing to perform a notarial act. As a public servant, a Notary should treat all people fairly and equally.

Reasonable Care

Responsibility. As public servants, Notaries must act responsibly and exercise reasonable care in the performance of their official duties. If a Notary fails to do so, he or she may be subject to a civil suit to recover financial damages caused by the Notary's error or omission.

In general, reasonable care is the degree of concern and attentiveness a person of normal intelligence and responsibility would exhibit. If a Notary can show to a judge or jury that he or she did everything expected of a reasonable person, the judge or jury is obligated by law to find the Notary blameless and not liable for damages.

Complying with all pertinent laws is the first rule of reasonable care for a Notary. If there are no statutory guidelines in a given instance, the Notary should go to extremes to use common sense and prudence. (See "Steps to Proper Notarization," pages 12–16.)

Unauthorized Practice of Law

Do Not Assist with Legal Matters. A Notary may not give legal advice or accept fees for legal advice. As a ministerial officer, a nonattorney Notary generally is not permitted to assist in drafting, preparing, selecting, completing or explaining a document or transaction (TGC, Sec. 406.017 and NPEM).

The Notary should not fill in blank spaces in the text of a document for other persons, tell others what documents they need nor how to draft them, nor advise others about the legal sufficiency of a document — and especially not for a fee.

A Notary, of course, may fill in the blanks on the portion of a document containing the notarial wording. And a Notary, as a private individual, may prepare legal documents to which he or she is personally a party; but the Notary may not then notarize his or her signature on those same documents.

Notaries who overstep their authority by advising others on legal matters may have their commissions revoked and may be prosecuted for the unauthorized practice of law.

Do Not Determine Notarial Act. A Notary who is not an attorney may not determine the type of notarial act to perform or decide which certificate to attach. This is beyond the scope of the Notary's expertise and might be considered the unauthorized practice of law. The Notary should only follow instructions provided by the document, its signer, its issuing agency or its receiving agency, or by an attorney (NPEM).

If a document lacks notarial certificate wording, the Notary must ask the document signer what type of notarization — acknowledgment or jurat — is required. The Notary may then type the appropriate notarial wording on the document or attach a loose certificate. If the signer does not know what type of notarization is required, the issuing or receiving agency should be contacted to determine the type of notarization required. This decision is never the Notary's to make unless the Notary also is an attorney.

Exceptions. Nonattorney Notaries who are specially trained, certified or licensed in a particular field (e.g., real estate, insurance, escrow) may advise others about documents in that field, but in no other. In addition, trained paralegals under the supervision of an attorney may advise others about documents in routine legal matters.

Signature by Mark

Mark Serves as Signature. A person who cannot sign his or her name because of illiteracy or a physical disability may instead use a mark — an "X" for example — as a signature, as long as there are witnesses to the making of the mark.

Witnesses for Notarization. For a signature by mark to be notarized, there must be two disinterested witnesses to the making of the mark (TCPRC, Sec. 121.011). Both witnesses should also sign the document, and one witness should write out the marker's name beside the mark. The two witnesses should be in addition to the Notary. It is recommended that a mark also be affixed in the Notary's journal, and that the witnesses also sign the journal.

Notarization Procedures. Because a properly witnessed mark is regarded as a legal signature, no special procedures are required. The marker must be positively identified, as must any other signer. A special certificate is suggested — see pages 85–86.

Signing for Person Physically Unable to Sign

A Texas Notary may sign the name of a person who is physically unable to grip and use a pen. This procedure will be of particular benefit to suddenly disabled individuals who had not appointed an attorney in fact to sign for them (TGC, Sec. 406.0165).

Such a proxy signature only may be affixed on a document that is presented for notarization and only if the Notary has been asked to affix such a signature by the disabled individual and if there is a witness present, in addition to the Notary, who has no financial interest in the transaction.

The disabled person may direct the Notary to sign on his or her behalf either orally or through some mechanical or electrical device that both the Notary and witness clearly can understand.

This procedure may only be used with persons who are physically unable to sign. It may not be used with a person who cannot sign because of illiteracy or who prefers to have another sign as a matter of convenience. It may not be used with documents that do not need notarization.

Identification of Signer. Both the disabled signer and the witness must be identified by the Notary either through personal knowledge, a credible identifying witness personally known to the Notary, or through an authorized ID card. Beneath the proxy signature, the Notary must write the following:

Signature affixed by Notary in the presence of _____ (name of witness), under Section 406.0165, Government Code.

Validity of Signature. A signature properly made using this procedure is as valid as if a normal signature had been made by the disabled individual.

Certificate. After the Notary affixes a proxy signature and the required short statement on the document, a normal notarial certificate may then be executed. As with any signer, the disabled person should be screened for identity, willingness and basic competence. However, the Notary should note the special circumstances in the journal entry.

Notarizing for Minors

Under Age 18. Generally, persons must reach the age of majority before they can handle their own legal affairs and sign documents for themselves. In Texas, the age of majority is 18. Normally, natural guardians (parents) or court-appointed guardians will sign on a minor's behalf. In certain cases, minors may lawfully sign documents and have their signatures notarized — minors engaged in business transactions or children serving as court witnesses, for example.

Include Age Next to Signature. When notarizing for a minor, the Notary should ask the young signer to write his or her age next to the signature on the document and in the journal. This will alert any interested party that the signer is a minor. The Notary is not required to verify the minor signer's age.

Identification. The method for identifying a minor is the same as that for an adult. However, determining the identity of a minor can be a problem, because minors often do not possess acceptable identification documents, such as driver's licenses or passports. If the minor does not have an acceptable ID, then the other methods of identifying signers must be used, either the Notary's personal knowledge of the minor or the oath of a credible identifying witness who can identify the minor. (See "Identifying Document Signers," pages 41–45.)

Authentication

Documents Sent Out of State. Documents notarized in Texas
and sent out of state may be required to bear proof that the
Notary's signature and stamp are genuine and that the Notary had
authority to act at the time of notarization. This process of proving
the genuineness of an official signature and stamp is called
authentication or legalization.

In Texas, the proof is in the form of an authenticating
certificate attached to the notarized document by the Secretary
of State's Notary Public Unit. These authenticating certificates are
known by many different names: certificates of official character,
certificates of authority, certificates of capacity, certificates of
prothonotary, and "flags."

The fee for an authenticating certificate is $15 per document
(check or money order, payable to "Secretary of State"). The
certificate may be obtained by mail by writing to: "Secretary
of State," Notary Public Unit, P.O. Box 13375, Austin, Texas
78711-3375. You may also obtain a certificate in person from:
Secretary of State, Notary Public Unit, 1019 Brazos, Austin,
Texas, 78701.

The notarized document must be forwarded along with a
written request stating the name of the state where the document
will be filed, the Notary's name and commission expiration date,
and the fee. It is not the Notary's responsibility to pick up or pay
for the certificate of authority.

Documents Sent Out of Country. If a notarized document will
be sent out of the United States, a chain-authentication process
may be necessary and additional certificates of authority may have
to be obtained from the U.S. Department of State and different
ministries of a given foreign nation, here and abroad. This chain-
certification process can be time-consuming and expensive.

Apostilles and the Hague Convention. More than 90 nations,
including the United States, subscribe to a treaty under auspices
of the Hague Conference that simplifies authentication of
notarized documents exchanged between any of these nations.
The official name of this treaty, adopted by the Conference
on October 5, 1961, is the *Hague Convention Abolishing the
Requirement of Legalization for Foreign Public Documents*. (For a
list of the subscribing countries, see "Hague Convention Nations,"
pages 133–135.)

Under the Hague Convention, only one authenticating certificate, called an apostille, is necessary to ensure acceptance of a Notary's signature and stamp in these subscribing countries. (*Apostille* means "notation" in French.)

In Texas, *apostilles* are issued by the Secretary of State for a fee of $15 per document. The procedure is the same as for obtaining an ordinary authenticating certificate, and the country for which the document is destined also should be specified.

Apostilles Issued for Foreign Adoptions. The fee for an *apostille* issued in connection with proceedings related to the adoption of a child in another country is $10 per document and a maximum fee of $100 for all *apostilles* requested in connection with proceedings for the adoption of one child (TGC, Sec. 405.031).

Foreign Languages

Non-English Advertising. A nonattorney Notary advertising notarial services in a foreign language must take steps to guard against misinterpretation of his or her function as a Notary. Notaries are required to include in any such foreign language advertisement, whether printed or on radio or television, the following in both English and the foreign language (TGC, Sec. 406.017):

- The statement: "I am not an attorney licensed to practice law in Texas and may not give legal advice or accept fees for legal advice."

- The fees a Notary is allowed to charge.

The above applies to signs and all other forms of written communication (e.g., business cards, stationery).

Further, use of the term *notario* or *notario publico* to advertise notarial service is prohibited. First-time violators of this section are guilty of a Class A misdemeanor; for repeat offenders it is a third degree felony (TGC, Sec. 406.017).

Foreign-Language Documents. Ideally, documents in foreign languages should be referred to Texas Notaries who read and write those languages. If not available in the general public, bilingual Notaries often may be found in foreign consulates.

Texas law does not directly address notarizing documents written in a language the Notary cannot read. Although notarizing such documents is not expressly prohibited, there are difficulties and dangers in notarizing any document the Notary cannot understand. The foremost danger is that the document may have been misrepresented to the Notary. The Notary cannot know if the document is false or endorses or promotes a product using the Notary seal and may unknowingly perform an illegal act or facilitate fraud by notarizing it.

If a Notary chooses to notarize a document that he or she cannot read, at the very least the notarial certificate should be in English, or in a language the Notary can read.

Foreign-Language Signers. There should always be direct communication between the Notary and document signer — whether in English or any other language. The Notary should never rely on an intermediary or interpreter to be assured that a signer is willing, competent, and understands the transaction, since this third party may have a motive for misrepresenting the circumstances to the Notary and/or the signer.

Immigration

Do Not Give Advice. Nonattorney Notaries never may advise others on the subject of immigration, nor help others prepare immigration documents — and especially not for a fee. Notaries who offer immigration advice to others may be prosecuted for the unauthorized practice of law (TGC, Sec. 406.017).

Documents. Affidavits are the forms issued or accepted by the U.S. Citizenship and Immigration Services (USCIS) that might require notarization. Documents not issued by the USCIS are often notarized and submitted in support of an immigration or naturalization petition. These might include translator's declarations, statements from employers and banks and affidavits of relationship.

If there appears to be no room for the Texas Notary seal on an USCIS-issued document, federal officials advise it may be affixed over boilerplate text (standard clauses or sections).

Naturalization Certificates. A Notary may be in violation of federal law if he or she makes a typewritten, photostatic or any other copy of a certificate of naturalization or notarizes it (U.S. Penal Code, Sec. 75 and U.S. Code, Title 18, Sec. 137).

Military-Officer Notarizations

<u>May Notarize Worldwide</u>. Certain U.S. military officers may notarize anywhere in the world for military personnel and other associated groups stipulated by the U.S. Code, Title 10, Subtitle A, Part II, Chapter 53, Section 1044a. Based on that code, the following persons are authorized to act as Notaries:

• Civilian attorneys serving as legal assistance attorneys

• Judge advocates, including reserve judge advocates when not in a duty status

• Adjutants, assistant adjutants and personnel adjutants, including reserve members when not in a duty status

• Other members of the armed forces, including reserve members when not in a duty status, so authorized by armed-forces regulations, by the regulations of the relevant Secretary or by statute

<u>Validity of Notarial Acts</u>. The signature of any of the above when acting as a Notary, together with the title of that individual's office, is considered proof that the signature is genuine, that the individual holds the designated title and that the individual is authorized to perform notarial acts. In such military-officer notarizations, failure to affix an official seal does not invalidate the acknowledgment or proof (USC Title 10, Section 1044a and TCPRC, Sec. 121.001).

<u>Fees</u>. Military-officer Notaries may not charge or receive a fee for performing a notarial act (USC Title 10, Section 1044a).

Wills

<u>Do Not Offer Advice</u>. Often, people attempt to draw up wills on their own without benefit of legal counsel and then bring these homemade testaments to a Notary to have them "legalized," expecting the Notary to know how to proceed. In advising or assisting such persons, the Notary risks prosecution for the unauthorized practice of law. The Notary's ill-informed advice may do considerable damage to the affairs of the signer and subject the Notary to a civil lawsuit to recover losses.

Wills are highly sensitive documents, the format of which is strictly dictated by laws. The slightest deviation from these laws can nullify a will. In some cases, holographic (handwritten) wills have actually been voided by notarization because the document was not entirely in the handwriting of the testator.

Do Not Proceed Without Certificate Wording. A Notary should notarize a document described as a will only if a notarial certificate is provided or stipulated for each signer, and the signers are not asking questions about how to proceed. Any such questions should properly be answered by an attorney.

Living Wills. Documents popularly called living wills may be notarized. These are not actually wills at all, but written statements of the signer's wishes concerning medical treatment in the event that person has an illness or injury and is unable to issue instructions on his or her own behalf.

Advance Directives

Under the *Texas Health and Safety Code* (THSC), an "advance directive" is an instruction to administer, withhold, or withdraw life-sustaining treatment in the event of a terminal or irreversible condition, an out-of-hospital do-not-resuscitate order or a medical power of attorney. The law permits advance directives, and medical powers of attorney in particular, to be executed by the declarant before two witnesses or acknowledged before a Notary Public. Furthermore, the law permits an advance directive or a written revocation of an advance directive to be signed by the declarant, witnesses or Notary with an electronic or digital signature.

Electronic Signature. An "electronic signature" is a facsimile, scan, uploaded image, computer-generated image, or other electronic representation of a manual signature that is intended by the signer to have the same force and effect as a manual signature (THSC 166.002[5-b]). An electronic signature must meet the following criteria (THSC 166.011[a][2]):

- Is capable of verification

- Is under the sole control of the person using it

- Is linked to data in a manner that invalidates the electronic signature if the data is changed

- Persists with the document and not by association in separate files.

Digital Signature. A "digital signature" is an electronic identifier intended by the signer to have the same force and effect as a manual signature (THSC 166.002[5-a]). A digital signature must meet the following criteria (THSC 166.011[a][1]):

- Uses an algorithm approved by the Texas Department of State Health Services

- Is unique to the person using it
- Is capable of verification

- Is under the sole control of the person using it

- Is linked to data in a manner that invalidates the digital signature if the data is changed

- Persists with the document and not by association in separate files

- Is bound to a digital certificate.

Approved Algorithms. The Texas Department of State Health Services may consider an algorithm approved by the National Institute of Standards and Technology (THSC 166.011[b]).

Out-of-Hospital Do Not Resuscitate (DNR) Orders

DNR Validity. Responding health care professionals must determine that an out-of-hospital DNR order appears valid by ensuring that the DNR order meets the following requirements (HSC 166.089[d]):

- Is completed, signed and witnessed or acknowledged before a Notary, as applicable

- Is dated

- Is signed with a manual, digital or electronic signature.

Rulemaking. No later than December 10, 2009, the executive commissioner of the Health and Human Services Commission must publish rules and modify the advance directive forms as necessary in order to permit notarization of the forms and provide for the use of a digital or electronic signature (THSC 166.083[b][6]).

MISCONDUCT, FINES AND PENALTIES

Prohibited Acts

Unauthorized Practice of Law. A Notary may not give legal advice or accept fees for legal advice. As a ministerial officer, the nonattorney Notary generally is not permitted to assist other persons in drafting, preparing, selecting, completing or understanding a document or transaction (TGC, Sec. 406.016 and NPEM). (See "Unauthorized Practice of Law," pages 54–55.)

Failure to Affix Seal Impression. A Notary must not fail to attach a seal impression to any document he or she notarizes. An instrument missing the official seal will be considered invalid. A Notary may be subject to civil action by aggrieved parties (TGC, Sec. 406.054 and TCPRC, Sec. 121.014).

Issue Identification. A Notary may not issue identification cards or documents (TGC, Sec. 406.016).

Notarize Own Signature. Notaries are not permitted to notarize their own signatures (NPEM).

Notarize Under Another Name. A Notary must sign the name under which he or she was commissioned — the name that appears on the commission paper — to certify notarial acts. No other name may be used (NPEM).

Certify Copies of Recordable Documents. Texas Notaries may not certify copies of recordable documents or vital records. A document does not have to be recorded, but merely recordable for the Notary to be prohibited from making a certified copy. In addition to recordable documents and vital records, the Texas Secretary of State specifically prohibits Notaries from certifying copies of passports; Social Security cards; military IDs; visas; certificates of naturalization; other ID cards/documents issued by the US Dept of Homeland Security; wills; and college or high school transcripts or diplomas (TGC, Sec. 406.016, NPEM and Secretary of State Web site). (See "Certified Copies," pages 27–29.)

Failure to Require Personal Appearance. A Notary may not notarize any document without the signer personally appearing before the Notary (TGC, Sec. 406.009).

Overcharging. A Notary may not charge more than the maximum fees allowed by law. If a Notary charges more than the legally prescribed fees, the Notary may have his or her commission suspended or revoked by the Secretary of State (TGC, Sec. 406.024 and NPEM).

In addition, the Notary is liable to the person overcharged for four times the fee unlawfully demanded (TGC, Sec. 603.010).

Use of the Term *Notario Publico*. Notaries are prohibited from using the term *notario* or *notario publico* in any printed, radio or television ad for notarial services (TGC, Sec. 406.017).

Copy or Notarize Naturalization Certificates. It can be a serious violation of federal law to make a typewritten, photostatic or any other copy of a certificate of naturalization or notarize it. Severe penalties are prescribed, including imprisonment (U.S. Penal Code, Sec. 75 and U.S. Code, Title 18, Sec. 137).

Denial, Suspension or Revocation of Commission

Authority of Secretary of State. The Texas Secretary of State may, for good cause, suspend or revoke the commission of a Notary Public. In such case, the Notary has the right to be given notice, to have a hearing and to appeal (TGC, Sec. 406.009).

Application Misstatement. The Texas Secretary of State may deny a Notary commission to any applicant who submits an application containing a knowingly made false statement (TGC, Sec. 406.009).

Conviction of Felony or Crime of Moral Turpitude. A Notary who is convicted of a felony or crime involving moral turpitude may have his or her commission application denied by the Secretary of State (TGC, Sec. 406.009).

Violation of Notarial Law. A Notary who is convicted of violating a law concerning the regulation or conduct of Notaries in Texas or another state may have his or her commission application denied by the Secretary of State (TGC, Sec. 406.009).

Similarly, if a Notary receives an administrative, criminal or civil penalty for violation of a Notary rule or law, his or her commission application may be denied (TGC, Sec. 406.009).

Disposition of Records. If removed from office, the ex-Notary must deliver his or her journal and public papers to the clerk of the county in which the Notary resides (TGC, Sec. 406.022). (See "Disposition of Notary Records," page 48.)

Overcharging. If a Notary charges more than the legally prescribed fees, the Notary's commission may be suspended or revoked by the Secretary of State (TGC, Sec. 406.024 and NPEM). In addition, the Notary is liable to the person overcharged for four times the fee unlawfully demanded (TGC, Sec. 603.010).

Improper Foreign-Language Advertising. A nonattorney Notary who advertises notarial services in a language other than English and who fails to post the fees allowed by law and the required conspicuous notice in both English and in the foreign language may be guilty of a Class A misdemeanor for a first offense or, for a repeat violation, of a third-degree felony. In addition, the Secretary of State may revoke or suspend the commission (TGC, Secs. 406.009 and 406.017).

A Notary who literally translates the phrase "Notary Public" into Spanish (i.e., *notario publico* or *notaria publica*) may have his or her commission suspended or revoked (TGC, Sec. 406.009 and 406.017).

In addition to a violation of any other law, failure to comply with either of the preceding is a deceptive trade practice actionable under Chapter 17, Business and Commerce Code (TGC, Sec. 406.017).

Failure to Require Personal Appearance. A Notary who performs a notarization when the signer or oath taker does not personally appear before the Notary at the time of notarization may have his or her commission suspended or revoked by the Secretary of State (TGC, Sec. 406.009).

Neglect of Duty. A Notary who is found guilty of willful neglect of duty or malfeasance (misconduct) may be removed from office. A Notary who is indicted for and convicted of a willful neglect of duty or official misconduct shall be removed from office (TGC, Sec. 406.018).

Failure to Maintain Residency. If a Notary moves his or her residence out of Texas, he or she vacates the office of Notary. Such a move has the same effect as resignation (TGC, Sec. 406.020).

An *ex officio* Notary — one who acquires notarial powers because of a particular office or position — who moves permanently from his or her assigned jurisdiction vacates the office of Notary Public. Such a move has the same effect as resignation (TGC, Sec. 406.021).

Grounds Disallowed for Commission Denial, Suspension and Revocation. Effective September 1, 2009, the following grounds may not be considered as a conviction for the purposes of qualifying an applicant for a Notary commission or as good cause for rejecting an application for a commission or suspending or revoking the commission of a Notary (TGC 406.009):

- A dismissal of a proceeding

- A discharge before an adjudication of guilt

- A finding of guilt that has been set aside

Civil Lawsuit

Liable for All Damages. A person injured by the failure, refusal or neglect of a Notary may sue to recover damages (TCPRC, Sec. 121.014).

As a ministerial official, a Texas Notary is liable for all damages caused by any intentional or unintentional misconduct or neglect. The $10,000 bond offers no protection to the Notary, since the Notary will be required to reimburse the bonding firm for any funds paid out to a victim of the Notary's misconduct. A civil lawsuit against the Notary may seek financial recovery for the full extent of damages (NPEM).

Notary errors and omissions insurance, on the other hand, does provide protection for a Notary who is sued for damages resulting from unintentional mistakes made while performing notarial acts. Such insurance is optional and is available from many sources. Errors and omissions insurance does not cover the Notary for intentional misconduct.

Appeal of Penalty

Hearing. A Notary whose commission has been suspended or revoked by the Secretary of State has rights to notice, hearing, adjudication and appeal. An appeal is to the District Court of Travis County. The Secretary of State has the burden of proof, and the trial is conducted as if there were no previous judgment (TGC, Sec. 406.009).

ELECTRONIC NOTARIZATION

Uniform Electronic Transactions Act

Electronic Signatures Acceptable. Through legislative enactment of Senate Bill 393 in 2001, Texas adopted the Uniform Electronic Transactions Act (UETA), which allows legal use of "electronic signatures" if all parties to a transaction agree.

In particular, the UETA allows Texas Notaries to use electronic signatures in notarizing other electronic signatures:

If a law requires a signature or record to be notarized, acknowledged, verified, or made under oath, the requirement is satisfied if the electronic signature of the person authorized to perform those acts together with all other information required to be included by other applicable law, is attached to or logically associated with the signature or record (Business & Commerce Code, Sec. 43.011).

Uniform Real Property Electronic Recording Act

Electronic Real Property Documents. A Notary may use an electronic signature in notarizing an electronic real property document destined for recordation in a county electronic recording system (Texas Property Code [TPC] Sec. 15.004[c]).

Image of Seal Not Required. On an electronically notarized real property document, a physical or electronic image of a stamp, impression, or seal need not accompany an electronic signature (TPC, Sec. 15.004[c]).

Other Applicable Statutes

Advance Medical Directives. A Texas Notary may perform an electronic notarial act on an advance medical directive using an electronic or digital signature. (See "Advance Directives," pages 62–63.)

Seal Elements, But Not Seal Image Required. The image or form of the Notary's official physical seal is not required on an electronically transmitted authenticated document; however, the required elements of the Notary's physical seal must be reproduced (TGC Sec. 406.013[d]). ■

Test Your Knowledge

Trial Exam

Instructions. This examination is designed to test your knowledge of the basic concepts of notarization. Work through the exam without looking at the answers, then check your responses and note where you need additional study. Careful review of "Notary Laws Explained" (pages 17–68), the reprinted Notary statutes (pages 75–110), "10 Most-Asked Questions" (pages 7–11), and "Steps to Proper Notarization" (pages 12–16) will produce the answers.

A perfect score on this examination is 100 points. There are:

- Twenty true/false questions worth one point each.
- Five multiple-choice questions worth four points each.
- Five fill-in-the-blank questions worth four points each.
- Five essay questions worth eight points each.

Now, get a separate sheet of paper and a pen or pencil, and get ready to test your knowledge.

True/False. For the following statements, answer true or false. Each correct answer is worth one point:

1. Notaries may act only in the county where they are commissioned. True or false?

2. The maximum Notary fee for taking the acknowledgment of three signers is $15. True or false?

3. It is a Notary's duty to serve all persons requesting lawful notarial acts, even those who are not customers. True or false?

4. Notaries must keep a photocopy of every document notarized. True or false?

5. A deposition is oral testimony that is written down and used as evidence in a court proceeding. True or false?

6. Notaries can withhold their services if they believe a signer is unable to understand a document. True or false?

7. It is a Notary's duty to draft powers of attorney, mortgages and deeds, upon request. True or false?

8. The letters "L.S." stand for the Latin words *locus sigilli*, which mean "location of the seal." True or false?

9. Holographic wills must be notarized to be valid. True or false?

10. A credible witness vouches for the identity of a signer in the Notary's presence and a subscribing witness for the identity of a signer out of the Notary's presence. True or false?

11. Notaries may notarize documents executed by the company that employs them. True or false?

12. A Notary who does not charge fees is not required to keep a journal. True or false?

13. The Notary needn't reimburse the surety company for bond funds paid out to a person financially harmed by the Notary's actions. True or false?

14. A Notary may not investigate whether a signer does indeed have authority to sign as a corporate officer. True or false?

15. A Notary's seal and journal belong to the Notary's employer if the employer paid for them. True or false?

16. An acknowledgment certificate is not to be used for jurats or proofs of execution by a subscribing witness. True or false?

17. An affirmation is the legal equivalent of an oath, but has no reference to a Supreme Being. True or false?

18. If presented with a document that does not include notarial wording, the Notary should attach and complete an acknowledgment. True or false?

19. Notaries may not refuse to notarize blank or incomplete documents if they are signed in the Notary's presence. True or false?

20. A Notary may notarize a deed for a spouse. True or false?

Multiple Choice. Choose the one best answer to each question. Each correct answer is worth four points.

1. A Notary has a disqualifying interest when acting as...
a. A legal secretary typing papers under the instruction of an employer-attorney for a client.
b. A bank employee preparing loan documents.
c. A real estate agent selling a condominium.

2. To become a Notary, an applicant must...
a. Have been a state resident for at least one year.
b. Be at least 18 years old.
c. Pass an oral exam given by the governor's office.

3. A certificate of authority for a Notary may be obtained...
a. From the Governor's office or the County Clerk.
b. From a stationery store or the Notary himself/herself.
c. From the Secretary of State.

4. "Satisfactory evidence" of identity means reliance on...
a. ID cards or a credible witness.
b. ID cards or personal knowledge of identity.
c. A credible witness or personal knowledge of identity.

5. A Texas Notary may...
a. Take depositions and affidavits.
b. Correct obvious errors in the document being notarized.
c. Certify a copy of a foreign birth certificate.

Fill In the Blank. Write in the word or phrase that best completes each sentence. Each correct answer is worth four points.

1. The Notary and the Notary's _____ are liable for the Notary's neglect or official misconduct.

2. A solemn, spoken pledge that is not an affirmation is called an _____.

3. An acceptable ID card should contain a signature and a _____ of its bearer.

4. A certified copy certifies the _____ of the reproduction.

5. Wills written entirely in the testator's own handwriting are called _____.

Essay. Reply to each question or statement with a short paragraph. Each complete and correct response is worth eight points.

1. Discuss the distinctions between a Notary bond and Notary errors and omissions insurance.

2. How does a proof of acknowledgment by subscribing witness work?

3. What is an *apostille* and when is it used?

4. Why should a Notary always complete the journal entry before filling out a notarial certificate?

5. Outline the differences between an acknowledgment certificate and a jurat.

Test Answers

True/False. 1. F; 2. F; 3. T; 4. F; 5. T; 6. T; 7. F; 8. T; 9. F; 10. T; 11. T; 12. F; 13. F; 14. F; 15. F; 16. T; 17. T; 18. F; 19. F; 20. F

Multiple Choice. 1. c; 2. b; 3. c; 4. a; 5. a

Fill In The Blank. 1. Surety; 2. Oath; 3. Photograph; 4. Accuracy; 5. Holographic

Essay. Responses should include the basic information in the paragraphs below:

1. A Notary bond, obtained through a state-licensed surety company, provides protection for the public in case of the Notary's negligence or intentional misconduct. Up to the cash limit of the bond, the surety agrees to pay damages to anyone who suffers a loss because of the Notary's actions; the Notary, however, must reimburse the surety. Notary errors and omissions insurance, also purchased from a state-licensed company, protects the Notary in case of an unintentional error, up to the policy limit. The Notary does not reimburse the insurance company. A bond is required by law; errors and omissions insurance is not.

2. A proof of acknowledgment in lieu of an acknowledgment is sometimes used when a document's principal signer is unavailable to appear before a Notary. In most such cases, the principal will be out of town, out of state, or even out of the country. A subscribing witness who has either seen the principal sign the document or taken the principal's acknowledgment of the signature may present this document to a Notary on the principal's behalf. The witness must sign (subscribe) the document in addition to the principal. The witness, who must be personally known to the Notary, is given an oath by the Notary. A person who is a grantee or beneficiary of a document should not serve as a subscribing witness.

3. An *apostille* is a certificate authenticating the signature and seal of a Notary. It is issued under provisions of an international treaty, signed by more than 90 nations, called the *Hague Convention Abolishing the Requirement of Legalization for Foreign Public Documents.* For notarized documents exchanged between the subscribing nations, this treaty streamlines the time-consuming authentication process known as "chain certification" by requiring only one authenticating certificate, the *apostille* (French for "notation"). *Apostilles* for Texas Notaries are issued by the Secretary of State.

4. Filling out a journal entry before completing a notarial certificate prevents a signer from grabbing the document and leaving before an important record of the notarization is made in the journal.

5. An acknowledgment certificate certifies that the signer of
the document personally appeared before the Notary on
the date and in the county indicated. It also certifies that
the signer's identity was satisfactorily proven to the Notary
and that the signer acknowledged having signed freely. A
jurat certifies that the person signing the document did so in
the Notary's presence, that the person appeared before the
Notary on the date and in the county indicated, and that the
Notary administered an oath or affirmation to the signer. For
a jurat, it is also advisable to positively identify the signer.

Tally Your Score

After checking your answers, add up your score. Then look at
the grading scale below to determine how you stand:

- 90–100:   Excellent!
- 80–89:   Good, but some review needed.
- 70–79:   Fair. Reread the parts of the *Primer* covering the
answers you missed.
- Below 70: Below par. Study the laws thoroughly again. ■

Texas Laws Pertaining to Notaries Public

Reprinted on the following pages are the *Notary Public Education Materials* issued to newly commissioned Notaries by the Secretary of State. Also reprinted are the pertinent parts of Texas statutes affecting Notaries and notarial acts. These laws include legislation in effect starting September 1, 1997.

NOTARY PUBLIC EDUCATION MATERIALS

 Secretary of State
Notary Public Unit
P.O. Box 13375
Austin, TX 78711-3375

Foreword

The following educational materials are provided to you in accordance with Tex. Gov't Code Ann. § 406.008. Updated information or changes to this information may be found on the Internet at http://www.sos.state.tx.us/statdoc/edinfo.shtml.

This information should be kept for reference throughout your four-(4) year term. Please read through this information at least once before you begin to notarize in order to familiarize yourself with the responsibilities of your office.

THE STATUTES REFERRED TO IN THESE MATERIALS ARE SUBJECT TO LEGISLATIVE CHANGE. The Secretary of State will provide a copy of these changes only upon request. Contact the Secretary of State, Notary Public Unit, P.O. Box 13375, Austin, Texas 78711-3375 or call (512) 463-5705 following each legislative session.

The Secretary of State's office would like to thank the Texas Young Lawyers Association for permitting us to use excerpts from their former publication, *Texas Notary Public Handbook*.

Table of Contents*

Introduction

A Notary Public is a public servant with statewide jurisdiction who is authorized to take acknowledgments, protest instruments permitted by law to be protested (primarily negotiable instruments and bills and notes), administer oaths, take depositions, and certify copies of documents not recordable in the public records.

A Notary Public is, in the true sense of the word, "a public servant" and "an officer of the State of Texas", conveniently located in the community so that he/she may be of service to the public. Each Notary Public takes an official oath of office to faithfully perform the duties of the office, and to insure such performance is required to post a $10,000.00 bond with the Secretary of State.

The primary duty of a Notary Public is to show a disinterested party (the Notary Public) has admonished the signer of an instrument as to the importance of such a document, and the signer of such document has declared that his/her identity, his/her signature and his/her reasons for signing such an instrument are genuine. The signature and seal of a Notary Public do not prove these facts conclusively, but do provide prima facie proof of them, and allow persons in trade and commerce to rely upon the

---

* Page numbers refer to the pages in this *Primer*. Page numbers will differ in the actual *Notary Public Education Materials*.

truth and veracity of the Notary Public as a third party who has no personal interest in the transaction.

A Notary Public is personally liable for negligence or fraud in the performance of the duties of the office. The bond is to insure that the person injured can recover at least $10,000.00, but this does not protect the Notary Public from personal liability for the full extent of damages caused by a breach of official duty. In addition to civil liability, Notaries Public may be subject to criminal prosecution and the revocation or suspension of their Notary Public commission by the Secretary of State's office.

The Secretary of State's office may revoke or suspend the commission of any Notary Public for good cause subject to Tex. Gov't Code Ann. § 406.009 and the Notary Public rules. A high standard of conduct should always be maintained by a Notary Public.

Statutes

RECORD BOOK AND PUBLIC RECORDS

Tex. Gov't Code Ann. § 406.014 requires that a Notary Public maintain a record book. This record book must be maintained whether or not any fees are charged for your notary public services.

A notary public other than a court clerk notarizing instruments for the court shall keep in a book a record of: (1) the date of each instrument notarized; (2) the date of the notarization; (3) the name of the signer, grantor, or maker; (4) the signer's, grantor's, or maker's residence or alleged residence; (5) whether the signer, grantor, or maker is personally known by the notary public, was identified by an identification card issued by a governmental agency or a passport issued by the United States, or was introduced to the notary public and, if introduced, the name and residence or alleged residence of the individual introducing the signer, grantor, or maker; (6) if the instrument is proved by a witness, the residence of the witness, whether the witness is personally known by the notary public or was introduced to the notary public and, if introduced, the name and residence of the individual introducing the witness; (7) the name and residence of the grantee; (8) if land is conveyed or charged by the instrument, the name and residence of the original grantee and the county where the land is located; and (9) a brief description of the instrument. Entries in the notary's book are public information. A notary public shall, on payment of all fees, provide a certified copy of any record in the notary public's office to any person requesting the copy.

NOTARY SEAL

Tex. Gov't Code Ann. § 406.013 requires a Notary Public to use a seal of office to authenticate the Notary Public's acts. A printed seal does not mean a hand drawn seal.

(a) A notary public shall provide a seal of office that clearly shows, when embossed, stamped, or printed on a document, the words, "Notary Public, State of Texas" around a star of five points, the notary public's name, and the date the notary public's commission expires. The notary public shall authenticate all his official acts with the seal of office.

(b) The seal may be a circular form not more than two inches in diameter or a rectangular form not more than one inch in width and 2½ inches in length. The seal must have a serrated or milled edge border.

(c) The seal must be affixed by a seal press or stamp that embosses or prints a seal that legibly reproduces the required elements of the seal under photographic methods. An indelible ink pad must be used for affixing by a stamp the impression on an instrument to authenticate the notary public's official act.

(d) Subsection (c) does not apply to an electronically transmitted authenticated document, except that an electronically transmitted authenticated document must legibly reproduce the required elements of the seal.

CHANGE OF ADDRESS

Tex. Gov't Code Ann. § 406.019 requires a Notary Public to notify the Secretary of State of any change of address within ten (10) days of the date on which the change is made. You may fill out a Notary Public Change of Address form or send a letter with your name, social security number, old address, and new address to: Secretary of State, Notary Public Unit, P.O. Box 13375, Austin, Texas 78711-3375.

UNAUTHORIZED PRACTICE OF LAW

Tex. Gov't Code Ann. § 406.017 requires a Notary Public who is not an attorney and who advertises in a language other than English to post or include with the advertisement a notice that the Notary Public is not an attorney. This section also prohibits the use of "Notario Publico".

An attorney or similar trained legal professional often holds the position of a Notary Public in Mexico and many foreign countries. To avoid deception by such persons and to dispel erroneous assumptions, the Texas Legislature enacted Section 406.017 to prescribe special provisions applicable to advertisements by a Notary Public in languages other than English.

(a) A person commits an offense if the person is a notary public and the person:

(1) states or implies that the person is an attorney licensed to practice law in this state;

(2) solicits or accepts compensation to prepare documents for or otherwise represent the interest of another in a judicial or administrative proceeding, including a proceeding relating to immigration to the United States, United States citizenship, or related matters;

(3) solicits or accepts compensation to obtain relief of any kind on behalf of another from any officer, agency, or employee of this state or the United States;

(4) uses the phrase "notario" or "notario publico" to advertise the services of a notary public, whether by signs, pamphlets, stationery, or other written communication or by radio or television; or

(5) advertises the services of a notary public in a language other than English, whether by signs, pamphlets, stationery, or other written communication or by radio or television, if the person does not post or

otherwise include with the advertisement a notice that complies with Subsection (b).

(b) The notice required by Subsection (a)(5) must state that the notary public is not an attorney and must be in English and in the language of the advertisement and in letters of a conspicuous size. If the advertisement is by radio or television, the statement may be modified, but must include substantially the same message. The notice must include the fees that a notary public may charge and the following statement:

"I AM NOT AN ATTORNEY LICENSED TO PRACTICE LAW IN TEXAS AND MAY NOT GIVE LEGAL ADVICE OR ACCEPT FEES FOR LEGAL ADVICE."

(c) It is an exception to prosecution under this section that, at the time of the conduct charged, the person is licensed to practice law in this state and in good standing with the State Bar of Texas.

(d) Except as provided in Subsection (e) of this section, an offense under this section is a Class A misdemeanor.

(e) An offense under this section is a felony in the third degree if it is shown on the trial of the offense that the defendant has previously been convicted under this section.

(f) Failure to comply with this section is, in addition to a violation of any other applicable law of this state, a deceptive trade practice actionable under Chapter 17, Business & Commerce Code. (1987, ch. 147, sec. 1; 2001, ch. 566, sec. 1)

REVOCATION OR SUSPENSION OF COMMISSION BY THE SECRETARY OF STATE

Tex. Gov't Code Ann. § 406.009 gives the Secretary of State the authority to reject an application, or suspend or revoke the commission of any Notary Public for "good cause."

(a) The secretary of state may, for good cause, reject an application or suspend or revoke the commission of a notary public.

(b) An action by the secretary of state under this section is subject to the rights of notice, hearing, adjudication, and appeal.

(c) An appeal under this section is to the district court of Travis County. The secretary of state has the burden of proof, and the trial is conducted de novo.

(d) In this section, "good cause" includes:

(1) a final conviction for a crime involving moral turpitude;

(2) a false statement knowingly made in an application;

(3) the failure to comply with Section 406.017;

(4) a final conviction for a violation of a law concerning the regulation of the conduct of notaries public in this or another state;

(5) the imposition on the notary public of an administrative, criminal, or civil penalty for a violation of a law or rule prescribing the duties of a notary public; or

(6) performing any notarization when the person for whom the notarization is performed did not personally appear before the notary at the time the notarization is executed.

FEES POSTED

Section 603.008 of the Government Code requires a Notary Public to keep posted the fees that a Notary is authorized by law to charge.

A county judge, clerk of the district or county court, sheriff, justice of the peace, constable, or notary public shall keep posted at all times in a conspicuous place in the respective offices a complete list of fees the person may charge by law.

FEE BOOK

Section 603.006 of the Government Code requires a Notary Public who charges a fee for notary services to keep a fee book.

An officer who by law may charge a fee for a service shall keep a fee book and shall enter in the book all fees charged for services rendered.

TO ITEMIZE COSTS

Section 603.007 of the Government Code states that a Notary Public must itemize or be prepared to itemize the fees that the Notary charges for performing notarial services.

A fee under this chapter is not payable to a person until a clerk or officer produces, or is ready to produce, a bill in writing containing the details of the fee to the person who owes the fee. The bill must be signed by the clerk or officer to whom the fee is due or who charges the fee or by the successor in office or legal representative of the clerk or officer.

FEES

Tex. Gov't Code Ann. § 406.024 sets out the maximum fees a Notary Public, or its employer, may charge for their Notary Public services. A Notary Public who charges more than the maximum set out below subjects the Notary to possible criminal prosecution and suspension or revocation of the Notary's Notary Public commission by the Secretary of State's office.

Notaries Public may charge the following fees:

Protesting a bill or note for non-acceptance ornon-payment, register and seal...$4.00

Each notice of protest 1.00

Protesting in all cases..4.00

Certificate and seal to such protest 4.00

Taking the acknowledgment or proof of any deed or other instrument in writing, for registration, including certificate and seal:

   (1) for the first signature 6.00

   (2) for each additional signature...1.00

Administering an oath or affirmation with certificate and seal...........6.00

All certificates under seal not otherwise provided for 6.00

Copies of all records and papers in their office, for each page .... .50

Taking the depositions of witnesses, for each 100 words .... .50

Swearing a witness to depositions, making certificate therefore with seal, and all other business connected with taking such deposition..............6.00

All notarial acts not provided for...6.00

Questions Frequently Asked

The following section consists of questions Notaries Public often have about their office. If you have any questions about notarizing a document you should contact the maker of the document, the Notary Public Unit of the Secretary of State's office, or an attorney.

1. May I notarize my spouse's signature?

2. May I notarize for my spouse's business?

3. May I notarize for my relatives? The basic rules are: the act of taking and certifying acknowledgments cannot be performed by a Notary Public financially or beneficially interested in the transaction; and one who is a party to an instrument, cannot act as a Notary Public. There is no specific prohibition against a Notary Public notarizing another spouse's signature or a Notary Public notarizing for a spouse's business. The facts in each situation will determine whether such action is proper.

4. May I alter or change the instrument I notarize? To answer this question, a distinction must be made between the instrument and the acknowledgment. A Notary Public is not authorized to change, alter or draft any instrument. However, a Notary Public may correct the certificate of acknowledgment to reflect the proper facts. For example, if an acknowledgment is taken in Webb County and the certificate shows Marion County, the certificate may be corrected as follows:

The State of Texas
County of ~~Marion~~ Webb

Before me _____ (Notary Public's name), A Notary Public, on this day personally... etc.

5. May I perform notarial acts in other counties? Yes. A Notary Public has statewide jurisdiction and may perform notarial acts in any county in the state of Texas.

6. May I perform functions other than those outlined in Tex. Gov't Code § 406.016, and may I charge fees in excess of those authorized in Tex. Gov't Code § 406.024? No. Notary Public functions are statutorily stated and should be provided in accordance with the law prescribed. A Notary Public may not charge more than the prescribed fees for performance of notarial acts.

7. What if there is a difference between the date the instrument is signed and the date the acknowledgment is actually taken? To answer this question, an example is given. If an instrument ends with the wording: "Signed and executed at Tyler, Smith County, Texas this 25th day of October, 2001," and the party whose name appears on such instrument appears before the Notary Public on October 27, 2001, the Notary Public would fill in the acknowledgment with the true and correct date when the signer personally appeared before the Notary Public.

8. May I take an acknowledgment over the telephone? No. A Notary Public may not perform by telephone those notarial acts which require a personal appearance.

9. May I change my name from the name shown on my notary

public commission? Yes. A Notary Public may change the name on their commission by sending the Secretary of State a name change application, your current certificate of commission, a rider or endorsement from the insurance agency or surety, and a $20.00 filing fee. The above four elements must be sent in at the same time. For an instruction sheet, please contact the Notary Public Unit at 512-463-5705.

10. May I make a certified copy of a birth certificate or a marriage license? No. A birth certificate and marriage license are recordable documents. A recordable document is one that is recorded with some type of entity whether it be the Secretary of State's Office, a court of law, a county clerk, or the Bureau of Vital Statistics. Certified copies may be obtained by contacting such entities.

A non-recordable document is one that has not been nor will ever be recorded with any type of entity. For instance, a letter is not recorded with anyone but there are times the sender of the letter would like to maintain a certified copy of that letter for his or her file.

11. May a notary public determine which type of notarial certificate should be attached to a document? No. A Notary Public who is not an attorney should only complete a notarial certificate which is already on the document or type a certificate of the maker's choosing. If a Notary Public is brought a document without a certificate and decides which certificate to attach, that Notary Public would be "practicing law". However, a Notary Public is provided copies of sample notarial certificates with his or her Notary commission. The person for whom the notarization is performed may choose the certificate and, and the Notary may add such certificate to the document.

12. Should a notary public rely only on a credit card in determining the identification of a signer? No. If the signer is not personally known by the Notary Public or identified by a credible witness, the Notary Public must use an identification card issued by a governmental agency or a passport issued by the United States to identify the signer.

13. Is a Notary required to administer an oath to a deponent served a deposition upon written questions? Yes. A deposition upon written questions is to be taken before an officer authorized to administer oaths. Texas Rules of Civil Procedure, Rule 208. The officer is to administer the oath to the witness in the manner provided in Rule 204 of the Texas Rules of Civil Procedure. Rule 204(2) specifies that every person whose deposition is taken shall be first cautioned and sworn to testify the truth, the whole truth and nothing but the truth. The officer shall then take the testimony of the witness in response to the questions in the manner provided in Rule 204(3) of the Texas Rules of Civil Procedure. Under Rule 204(3), the witness shall be carefully examined, his/her testimony is to be recorded at the time it is given and thereafter transcribed by the officer taking the deposition or by some person under his/her personal supervision.

Prohibited Acts

THE SECTION BELOW PROVIDES A NOTARY PUBLIC WITH A LIST OF PROHIBITED ACTS THAT THE NOTARY MAY NOT DO IN CARRYING

OUT THE NOTARY'S OFFICE. IF THE NOTARY PUBLIC PERFORMS ANY
OF THE FOLLOWING, THE NOTARY MAY BE SUBJECTING THE NOTARY
TO POSSIBLE CRIMINAL PROSECUTION, CIVIL LIABILITY, AND THE
REVOCATION OR SUSPENSION OF THE NOTARY'S NOTARY PUBLIC
COMMISSION.

A Notary Public may not:

1. perform acts which constitute the practice of law, the performance
   thereof being restricted to licensed attorneys at law.
2. prepare, draft, select, or give advice concerning legal documents.
3. translate the term "Notary Public" into Spanish (Notario Publico).
4. overcharge for Notary Public services.
5. notarize a document without the signer being in the Notary's
   presence.
6. notarize the Notary's own signature.
7. issue identification cards.
8. sign a document under any other name than the one under which the
   Notary was commissioned.
9. fail to attach a Notary seal to any document that the Notary notarizes.
10 certify copies of documents recordable in the public records.

Notarial Definitions

Acknowledgment: A formal declaration before an authorized official,
by the person who executed the instrument, that it is the signer's free act
and deed. The certificate of the officer on such instrument that it has been
so acknowledged.

Affidavit: A written or printed declaration or statement of facts, made
voluntarily, confirmed by the oath or affirmation of the party making it, and
taken before a Notary Public or other officer having authority to administer
such oath. It is made either with or without notice to adverse parties thereto.

Affirmation: The act of affirming the truth of a document, not an oath.
"I solemnly affirm and declare the foregoing to be a true statement..." Note
that an affidavit may appear in two forms: a sworn affidavit with oath, or an
affirmed affidavit with affirmation. Each has the same legal import.

Jurat: The clause written at the foot of an affidavit or document stating
when, where and before whom such affidavit was sworn or affirmed. The
expiration date of the Notary Public's commission is commonly included.

Oath: An external pledge or affirmation, made in verification of
statements made or to be made, coupled with an appeal to a sacred or
venerated object, in evidence of the seriousness and reverent state of mind
of the party; an invocation to a supreme being to witness the words of the
party and to visit him with punishment if they be false.

Protest: A statement issued by a Notary Public that a certain bill or note
was presented for payment or acceptance, and such payment or acceptance
was refused. The Notary Public attests that the refuser shall be liable for any
losses arising from the dishonor of the document.

Verification: The ascertaining of an allegation to be true; the acceptance
of the Notary that the person appearing before the Notary has been properly

identified as being the person purported to be; to make sure of proper procedure and verify same; to give a verification over the Notary's official signature and seal where necessary to the transaction of the business.

Sample Forms

In the following examples, a personalized seal includes the words "Notary Public, State of Texas" around a star of five points, the Notary Public's name, and the date the Notary Public's commission expires.

ACKNOWLEDGMENTS

I. Ordinary Certificate

State of Texas
County of _____,

Before me, _____ (insert the name and character of the officer), on this day personally appeared _____, known to me (or proved to me on the oath of _____ or through _____ [description of identity card or other document]) to be the person whose name is subscribed to the foregoing instrument and acknowledged to me that he executed the same for the purposes and consideration therein expressed. Given under my hand and seal of office this _____ day of _____, _____(year).

_____
(PERSONALIZED SEAL)   Notary Public's Signature

II. Short Forms

A. For a natural person acting in his/her own right:

State of Texas
County of _____

This instrument was acknowledged before me on _____ (date) by _____ (name of person or persons acknowledging).

_____
(PERSONALIZED SEAL)   Notary Public's Signature

B. For a natural person as principal acting by attorney-in-fact:

State of Texas
County of _____

This instrument was acknowledged before me on _____ (date) by _____ (name of attorney-in-fact) as attorney-in-fact on behalf of _____ (name of principal).

_____
(PERSONALIZED SEAL)   Notary Public's Signature

C. For a partnership acting by one or more partners:

State of Texas
County of _____

This instrument was acknowledged before me on _____ (date)
by _____ (name of acknowledging partner or partners), partner(s) on
behalf of _____ (name of partnership), a partnership.

_____
(PERSONALIZED SEAL)   Notary Public's Signature

D. For a corporation:

State of Texas
County of _____

This instrument was acknowledged before me on _____ (date) by
 (name of officer), _____ (title of officer) of _____ (name
of corporation acknowledging), a _____ (state of incorporation)
corporation, on behalf of said corporation.

_____
(PERSONALIZED SEAL)   Notary Public's Signature

E. For a public officer, trustee, executor, administrator, guardian, or
    other representative:

State of Texas
County of _____

This instrument was acknowledged before me on _____ (date)
by _____ (name of representative) as _____ (title of
representative) of _____ (name of entity or person represented).

_____
(PERSONALIZED SEAL)   Notary Public's Signature

ACKNOWLEDGMENT OF A MARK
The person should place his mark on the instrument at the place
designated for his signature. The words "His Mark" and the person's name
should be printed near the mark. The making of the mark should be
witnessed by two disinterested persons, other than the Notary, with the
signatures of the witnesses appearing near the mark.

His Mark
John X Doe

_____
John Doe

WITNESS:
Signature:_____   Signature:_____
Address:_____   Address:_____

State of Texas
County of _____

Before me, (insert the name and character of the officer), on this day
personally appeared _____, known to me (or proved to me on the oath
of _____ or through [description of identity card or other document])
to be the person whose mark is made on the foregoing instrument and
acknowledged to me that he executed the same for the purposes and
consideration therein expressed.
Given under my hand and seal of office this _____ day of _____, (year).

_____
(PERSONALIZED SEAL)   Notary Public's Signature

JURAT

State of Texas
County of _____

Sworn to and subscribed before me on the _____ day of _____,
_____ (year), by (name of principal signer)

_____
(PERSONALIZED SEAL)   Notary Public's Signature

VERIFICATIONS

Form 1:

State of Texas
County of _____

_____, personally appeared before me, and being first duly sworn
declared that, he/she signed this application in the capacity designated, if
any, and further states that he/she has read the above application and the
statements therein contained are true

_____
(PERSONALIZED SEAL)   Notary Public's Signature

Form 2:

State of Texas
County of _____

Before me, a Notary Public, on this day personally appeared _____,
known to me to be the person whose name is subscribed to the foregoing
document and, being by me first duly sworn, declared that the statements
therein contained are true and correct.

_____
(PERSONALIZED SEAL)   Notary Public's Signature

OATH OR AFFIRMATION

State of Texas
County of _____

I, _____ (affiant), do solemnly swear (or affirm), that I will faithfully execute the duties of the office of _____ of the State of Texas, and will to the best of my ability preserve, protect, and defend the laws of the United States and of this State, so help me God.

_____
Signature of Affiant

Sworn to and subscribed before me by _____ (affiant) on this _____ day of _____, _____ (year).

_____

(PERSONALIZED SEAL)   Notary Public's Signature

STATEMENT OF ELECTED OFFICER

State of Texas
County of _____

I, _____ (affiant), do solemnly swear (or affirm), that I have not directly or indirectly paid, offered, promised to pay, contributed, or promised to contribute any money or thing of value, or promised a public office or employment for the giving or withholding of a vote at the election at which I was elected so help me God.
_____ Signature of Affiant
Sworn to and subscribed before me by _____ (affiant) on this _____ day of _____, _____ (year).

_____

(PERSONALIZED SEAL)   Notary Public's Signature

STATEMENT OF APPOINTED OFFICER

State of Texas
County of _____

I, _____ (name of affiant), do solemnly swear (or affirm), that I have not directly or indirectly paid, offered, promised to pay, contributed, or promised to contribute any money or thing of value, or promised a public office or employment, as a reward to secure my appointment or confirmation thereof, so help me God. _____Signature of Affiant
Sworn to and subscribed before me by _____ (affiant) on this _____ day of _____, _____ (year).

_____

(PERSONALIZED SEAL)   Notary Public's Signature

DEPOSITION

Certificate To Deposition Upon Written Questions

State of Texas
County of _____

(Plaintiff)   ) In the _____Court
v.   ) of _____ County, Texas
(Defendant)   ) Cause No. _____
I hereby certify that the foregoing answers of _____, the witness
forenamed, were signed and sworn to before me on _____ (date), by
said witness.

_____

(PERSONALIZED SEAL)   Notary Public's Signature

PROTESTS

(Insert bill or note or copy thereof)

United States of America
State of Texas
County of _____
Be it known that on the _____ day of _____, _____ (year), at the
request of _____ (name), of _____, I _____ (Notary
Public's name), a Notary Public duly commissioned and sworn, residing
in _____County, Texas, did present the original _____
(instrument), hereto attached, for $_____, with accrued interest
thereon of $_____, dated _____, and demanded payment (or
acceptance) thereof which was refused.
Whereupon I, at the request of the aforesaid _____, did protest, and
by these presents do protest, as well against the drawer, maker, endorsers,
and acceptors of said instruments as against all others whom it may concern,
for exchange, costs, charges, damages, and interest already incurred and
hereinafter to be incurred by reason of non-payment thereof. I further certify
that on _____ (date), notice in writing of the foregoing presentment,
demand, refusal and protest was given by _____ (persons and status)
by depositing notices thereof in the post office at _____, Texas, postage
paid, directed as follows: _____. I further certify that notices were left
as follows:
Notice left for _____ at _____
Notice left for _____ at _____
Each of the named places the reputed place of residence of the person for
whom the notice was left.
    In testimony whereof I have hereunto set my hand and affixed my seal of
office at _____ Texas, on _____ day of _____, _____ (year).

_____

(PERSONALIZED SEAL)   Notary Public's Signature

(List fees and expenses to include postage)

CERTIFIED COPY OF A NON-RECORDABLE DOCUMENT

State of Texas
County of _____

On this _____ day of _____, _____ (year), I certify that the preceding or attached document, and the duplicate retained by me as a notarial record, are true, exact, complete, and unaltered photocopies made by me of _____ (description of document), presented to me by the document's custodian, _____, (*held in my custody as a notarial record) and that, to the best of my knowledge, the photocopied document is neither a public record nor a publicly recordable document, certified copies of which are available from an official source other than a notary.

_____
(PERSONALIZED SEAL)   Notary Public's Signature

*This phrase would be inserted and the preceding phrase, "presented to me by the document's custodian", would be deleted in the event a person was requesting a certified copy of the Notary Public's journal.

PERTINENT STATUTES GOVERNING TEXAS NOTARIES

Texas Government Code
Title 4. Executive Branch
Subtitle A. Executive Officers
Chapter 406. Notary Public; Commissioner of Deeds
Subchapter A. Notary Public

Subchapter A. Notary Public

Sec. 406.001. Appointments. The secretary of state may appoint a notary public at any time. (1987, ch. 146, sec. 1)

Sec. 406.002. Term. The term of a notary public expires four years after the date the notary qualifies. (1987, ch. 147, sec. 1)

Sec. 406.003. Jurisdiction. A notary public has statewide jurisdiction. (1987, ch. 147, sec. 1)

Sec. 406.004. Eligibility. Each person appointed and commissioned as a notary public shall be at least 18 years of age and a resident of the State of Texas and must not have been convicted of a felony or crime involving moral turpitude. (1987, ch. 147, sec. 1)

Sec. 406.005. Appointment Procedure — Statement. (a) Each person to be appointed a notary public shall submit an application to the secretary of state on a form prescribed by the secretary of state. The application must satisfy the secretary of state that the applicant is qualified. The application must state:

(1) the applicant's name to be used in acting as a notary public;

(2) the applicant's post office address;

(3) the applicant's county of residence;

(4) the applicant's date of birth;

(5) the applicant's driver's license number or the number of other official state-issued identification; and

(6) the applicant's social security number.

(b) The applicant shall also execute the statement of officers as required by Section 1, Article XVI, Texas Constitution.

(c) The statement shall be signed and sworn to or affirmed by the applicant in the presence of a notary public or other person authorized to administer oaths in this state. (1987, ch. 147, sec. 1; 1995, ch. 719, sec. 2)

Sec. 406.006. Qualification. An individual qualifies by:

(1) properly completing the application form;

(2) executing the statement;

(3) providing the bond;

(4) paying the required filing fees; and

(5) meeting the eligibility requirements. (1987, ch. 147, sec. 1; 1989, ch. 406, sec. 1; 1995, ch. 719, sec. 3)

Sec. 406.007. Fees Paid to Secretary of State. (a) The applicant must submit to the secretary of state:

(1) a fee of $10 for approving and filing the bond of the notary public; and

(2) a fee of $1 to be appropriated to and used by the secretary of state only for hiring an investigator and for preparing and distributing the materials required to be distributed under Section 406.008.

(b) The secretary of state shall charge for use of the state a fee of $10 for a notary public commission. The applicant must pay the fee in advance to the secretary of state. (1987, ch. 147, sec. 1; 1989, ch. 4, sec. 2.14)

Sec. 406.008. Commission; Notary Materials. (a) Immediately after the qualification of a notary public, the secretary of state shall send notice of appointment along with a commission to the notary public. The commission is effective as of the date of qualification.

(b) When the commission is issued, the secretary of state shall supply the notary public with:

(1) materials outlining the powers and duties of the office;

(2) a list of prohibited acts; and

(3) sample forms for an acknowledgment, jurat, and verification and for the administering of an oath, protest, and deposition.

(c) Repealed by Acts 1995, 74th Leg., ch. 719, sec. 10, eff. Jan. 1, 1996. (1987, ch. 147, sec. 1; 1995, ch. 719, secs. 4, 10)

Sec. 406.009. Rejection of Appointment; Suspension or Revocation of Commission. (a) The secretary of state may, for good cause, reject an application or suspend or revoke the commission of a notary public.

(b) An action by the secretary of state under this section is subject to the rights of notice, hearing, adjudication, and appeal.

(c) An appeal under this section is to the district court of Travis County. The secretary of state has the burden of proof, and the trial is conducted de novo.

(d) In this section "good cause" includes:

(1) a final conviction for a crime involving moral turpitude;

(2) a false statement knowingly made in an application;

(3) the failure to comply with Section 406.017;

(4) a final conviction for a violation of a law concerning the regulation of the conduct of notaries public in this or another state;

(5) the imposition on the notary public of an administrative, criminal, or civil penalty for a violation of a law or rule prescribing the duties of a notary public; or

(6) performing any notarization when the person for whom the notarization is performed did not personally appear before the notary at the time the notarization was executed.

(e) The following may not be considered a conviction for the purposes of determining eligibility and good cause:

(1) a dismissal of a proceeding against the defendant and discharge of

the defendant before an adjudication of guilt; and

(2) a finding of guilt that has been set aside.

(1987, ch. 147, sec. 1; 1989, ch. 4, sec. 2.15; 1995, ch. 719, secs. 5, 8)

Sec. 406.010. Bond; Oath. (a) Each person to be appointed a notary public shall, before entering the official duties of office, execute a bond in the amount of $10,000 with a solvent surety company authorized to do business in this state as a surety. The bond must be approved by the secretary of state, payable to the governor, and conditioned on the faithful performance of the duties of office. The secretary of state has the authority to accept an electronic filing of the notary public bond if an agreement has been made with the surety company.

(b) The notary bond shall be deposited in the office of the secretary of state, is not void on first recovery, and may be sued on in the name of the injured party from time to time until the whole amount of the bond is recovered.

(c) A notary public, before entering on the duties of office, shall take the official oath required by Section 1, Article XVI, Texas Constitution.

(d) The oath shall be signed and sworn to or affirmed by the notary public in the presence of a notary public or other person authorized to administer oaths in this state. A notary public cannot execute his or her own oath of office.

(e) The secretary of state shall provide an oath of office form along with the commission and educational materials. (1987, ch. 147, sec. 1; 1995, ch. 719, sec. 7)

Sec. 406.011. Reappointment. (a) Not earlier than 90 days prior to the expiration date of the notary's term, a notary public may apply for reappointment on submission of a new application to the secretary of state.

(b) A notary public who is not reappointed on or before the expiration date of the term the notary public is serving will be appointed for a new term expiring four years from the date of qualification. (1987, ch. 147, sec. 1; 1995, ch. 719, sec. 8)

Sec. 406.012. Inspection of Records. All records concerning the appointment and qualification of the notary public shall be kept in the office of the secretary of state. The records are public information. (1987, ch. 147, sec. 1; 1989, ch. 4, sec. 2.16)

Sec. 406.013. Seal. (a) A notary public shall provide a seal of office that clearly shows, when embossed, stamped, or printed on a document, the words "Notary Public, State of Texas" around a star of five points, the notary public's name, and the date the notary public's commission expires. The notary public shall authenticate all official acts with the seal of office.

(b) The seal may be a circular form not more than two inches in diameter or a rectangular form not more than one inch in width and 2-1/2 inches in length. The seal must have a serrated or milled edge border.

(c) The seal must be affixed by a seal press or stamp that embosses or prints a seal that legibly reproduced the required elements of the seal under photographic methods. An indelible ink pad must be used for affixing by a stamp the impression of a seal on an instrument to authenticate the notary public's official act.

(d) Subsection (c) does not apply to an electronically transmitted authenticated document, except that an electronically transmitted authenticated document must legibly reproduce the required elements of the seal. (1987, ch. 147, sec. 1; 1989, ch. 4, sec. 2.71(d); 2001, ch. 95, sec. 2)

Sec. 406.014. Notary Records. (a) A notary public other than a court clerk notarizing instruments for the court shall keep in a book a record of:

(1) the date of each instrument notarized;

(2) the date of the notarization;

(3) the name of the signer, grantor, or maker;

(4) the signer's, grantor's, or maker's residence or alleged residence;

(5) whether the signer, grantor, or maker is personally known by the notary public, was identified by an identification card issued by a governmental agency or a passport issued by the United States, or was introduced to the notary public and, if introduced, the name and residence or alleged residence of the individual introducing the signer, grantor, or maker.

(6) if the instrument is proved by a witness, the residence of the witness, whether the witness is personally known by the notary public or was introduced to the notary public and, if introduced, the name and residence of the individual introducing the witness;

(7) the name and residence of the grantee;

(8) if land is conveyed or charged by the instrument, the name of the original grantee and the county where the land is located; and

(9) a brief description of the instrument.

(b) Entries in the notary's book are public information.

(c) A notary public shall, on payment of all fees, provide a certified copy of any record in the notary public's office to any person requesting the copy.

(d) A notary public who administers an oath pursuant to Article 45.01, Code of Criminal Procedure, is exempt from the requirement in Subsection (a) of recording that oath.

(e) A Notary Public may maintain the records required by Subsection (a) electronically in a computer or other storage device. (1987, ch. 147, sec. 1; 1989, ch. 4, sec. 2.17(a); 1989, ch. 406, sec. 2; 1989, ch. 451, sec. 1)

Sec. 406.015. Copies Certified by County Clerk. (a) A copy of a record, declaration, protest, or other official act of the notary public may be certified by the county clerk with whom the instrument is deposited.

(b) A copy of an instrument certified by the county clerk under Subsection (a) has the same authority as if certified by the notary public by whom the record, declaration, protest, or other official act was originally made. (1987, ch. 147, sec. 1))

Sec. 406.016. Authority. (a) A notary public has the same authority as the county clerk to:

(1) take acknowledgments or proofs of written instruments;

(2) protest instruments permitted by law to be protested;

(3) administer oaths;

(4) take depositions; and

(5) certify copies of documents not recordable in the public records.

(b) A notary public shall sign an instrument in Subsection (a) in the name under which the notary public is commissioned.

(c) A notary public may not issue an identification card.

(d) A notary public not licensed to practice law in this state may not give legal advice or accept fees for legal advice. (1987, ch. 147, sec. 1)

Sec. 406.0165. Signing Document for Individual with Disability. (a) A notary may sign the name of an individual who is physically unable to sign or make a mark on a document presented for notarization if directed to do so by that individual, in the presence of a witness who has no legal or equitable interest in any real or personal property that is the subject of, or is affected by, the document being signed. The notary shall require identification of the witness in the same manner as from an acknowledging person under Section 121.005, Civil Practices and Remedies Code.

(b) A notary who signs a document under this section shall write, beneath the signature, the following or a substantially similar sentence:

"Signature affixed by notary in the presence of (name of witness), a disinterested witness, under Section 406.0165, Government Code."

(c) A signature made under this section is effective as the signature of the individual on whose behalf the signature was made for any purpose. A subsequent bona fide purchaser for value may rely on the signature of the notary as evidence of the individual's consent to execution of the document.

(d) In this section, "disability" means a physical impairment that impedes the ability to sign or make a mark on a document. (1997, ch. 1218, sec. 1)

Sec. 406.017. Representation as Attorney. (a) A person commits an offense if the person is a notary public and the person:

(1) states or implies that the person is an attorney licensed to practice law in this state;

(2) solicits or accepts compensation to prepare documents for or .... otherwise represent the interest of another in a judicial or administrative proceeding, including a proceeding relating to immigration to the United States, United States citizenship, or related matters;

(3) solicits or accepts compensation to obtain relief of any kind on .... behalf of another from any officer, agency, or employee of this state or the United States;

(4) uses the phrase "notario" or "notario publico" to advertise the .... services of a notary public, whether by signs, pamphlets, stationery, or other written communication or by radio or television; or

(5) advertises the services of a notary public in a language other than English, whether by signs, pamphlets, stationery, or other written communication or by radio or television, if the person does not post or otherwise include with the advertisement a notice that complies with Subsection (b).

(b) The notice required by Subsection (a)(5) must state that the notary public is not an attorney and must be in English and in the language of the advertisement and in letters of a conspicuous size. If the advertisement is by radio or television, the statement may be modified, but must include substantially the same message. The notice must include the fees that a notary public may charge and the following statement:

"I AM NOT AN ATTORNEY LICENSED TO PRACTICE LAW IN TEXAS AND MAY NOT GIVE LEGAL ADVICE OR ACCEPT FEES FOR LEGAL ADVICE."

(c) It is an exception to prosecution under this section that, at the time of the conduct charged, the person is licensed to practice law in this state and in good standing with the State Bar of Texas.

(d) Except as provided in Subsection (e) of this section, an offense under this section is a Class A misdemeanor.

(e) An offense under this section is a felony in the third degree if it is shown on the trial of the offense that the defendant has previously been convicted under this section.

(f) Failure to comply with this section is, in addition to a violation of any other applicable law of this state, a deceptive trade practice actionable under Chapter 17, Business & Commerce Code. (1987, ch. 147, sec. 1; 2001, ch. 566, sec. 1)

Sec. 406.018. Removal from Office. (a) A notary public guilty of wilful neglect of duty or malfeasance in office may be removed from office in the manner provided by law.

(b) A notary public indicted for and convicted of a wilful neglect of duty or official misconduct shall be removed from office. The court shall include the order for removal as part of its judgment. (1987, ch. 147, sec. 1)

Sec. 406.019. Change of Address. A notary public shall notify the secretary of state of a change of the notary public's address not later than the 10th day after the date on which the change is made. (1987, ch. 147, sec. 1)

Sec. 406.020. Removal from State. A notary public who removes his residence from this state vacates the office. (1987, ch. 147, sec. 1)

Sec. 406.021. Removal from Precinct. An ex officio notary public who moves permanently from the notary public's precinct vacates the office. (1987, ch. 147, sec. 1)

Sec. 406.022. Effect of Vacancy. If the office of a notary public becomes vacant due to resignation, removal, or death, the county clerk of the county in which the notary public resides shall obtain the record books and public papers belonging to the office of the notary public and deposit them in the county clerk's office. (1987, ch. 147, sec. 1; 1989, ch. 406, sec. 3)

Sec. 406.023. Administration and Enforcement. (a) The secretary of state shall adopt rules necessary for the administration and enforcement of this subchapter. The rules must be consistent with the provisions of this subchapter.

(b) The secretary of state may employ an investigator to aid in the enforcement of this subchapter.

(c) The secretary of state may provide for the appointment of county clerks as deputy custodians for the limited authentication of notary public records deposited in the clerks' offices. (1987, ch. 147, sec. 1)

Sec. 406.024. Fees Charged by Notary Public. (a) A notary public may charge the following fees:

(1) for protesting a bill or note for nonacceptance or nonpayment, register and seal, a fee of $4;

(2) for each notice of protest, a fee of $1;

(3) for protesting in all other cases, a fee of $4;

(4) for certificate and seal to a protest, a fee of $4;

(5) for taking the acknowledgment or proof of a deed or other instrument in writing, for registration, including certificate and seal, a fee of $6 for the first signature and $1 for each additional signature;

(6) for administering an oath or affirmation with certificate and seal, a fee of $6;

(7) for a certificate under seal not otherwise provided for, a fee of $6;

(8) for a copy of a record or paper in the notary public's office, a fee of 50 cents for each page;

(9) for taking the deposition of a witness, 50 cents for each 100 words;

(10) for swearing a witness to a deposition, certificate, seal, and other business connected with taking the deposition, a fee of $6; and

(11) for a notarial act not provided for, a fee of $6.

(b) A notary public may charge a fee only for an acknowledgment or official act under Subsection (a). The fee charged may not exceed the fee authorized by Subsection (a). (1987, ch. 147, sec. 1; 1989, ch. 4, sec. 2.18(a); 1995, ch. 259, sec. 1)

Sec. 406.025. Signature on Commission After Change in Office. If the governor or secretary of state ceases to hold or perform the duties of office, existing stocks of commissions bearing the person's printed name, signature, or facsimile signature may be used until they are exhausted, and the person succeeding to the office or the duties of the office shall have the commissions issued with:

(1) the obsolete printed name, signature, or facsimile signature struck through;

(2) the successor's printed name submitted for the obsolete printed name, signature, or facsimile signature; and

(3) the inscription "Printed name authorized by law" near the successor's printed name. (1995, ch. 719, sec. 9)

Subchapter B. Commissioner of Deeds

Sec. 406.051. Appointment. (a) The governor may biennially appoint and commission one or more individuals in other states, territories, or foreign countries or in the District of Columbia to serve as commissioner of deeds.

(b) An appointment may be made only on the recommendation of the executive authority of the state, territory, or foreign country or the District of Columbia. (1987, ch. 147, sec. 1)

Sec. 406.052. Term. The term of office of a commissioner of deeds is two years. (1987, ch. 147, sec. 1)

Sec. 406.053. Oath. Before performing the duties of office, a commissioner of deeds shall take and subscribe an oath to well and faithfully perform the duties of office under the laws of this state. The oath shall be:

(1) taken before the clerk of a court of record in the city, county, or country in which the commissioner resides;

(2) certified to by the clerk under the clerk's hand and seal of office; and

(3) filed in the office of the secretary of state of this state. (1987, ch. 147, sec. 1)

Sec. 406.054. Seal. A commissioner of deeds shall provide a seal with a star of five points in the center and the words "Commissioner of the State of Texas" engraved on the seal. The seal shall be used to certify all official acts of the commissioner of deeds. An instrument that does not have the impression of the seal, or an act of the commissioner of deeds that is not certified by the impression of the seal, is not valid in this state. (1987, ch. 147, sec. 1)

Sec. 406.055. Authority. A commissioner of deeds has the same authority as a notary public to take acknowledgments and proofs of written instruments, to administer oaths, and to take depositions to be used or recorded in this state. (1987, ch. 147, sec. 1)

Title 6. Public Officers and Employees
Subtitle A. Provisions Generally Applicable to Public Officer and Employees
Chapter 602. Administration of Oaths

Sec. 602.002. OATH MADE IN TEXAS. An oath made in this state may be administered and a certificate of the fact given by:

(1) a judge, retired judge, or clerk of a municipal court;

(2) a judge, retired judge, senior judge, clerk, or commissioner of a court of record;

(3) a justice of the peace or a clerk of a justice court;

(4) a notary public;

(5) a member of a board or commission created by a law of this state, in a matter pertaining to a duty of the board or commission;

(6) a person employed by the Texas Ethics Commission who has a duty related to a report required by Title 15, Election Code, in a matter pertaining to that duty;

(7) a county tax assessor-collector or an employee of the county tax assessor-collector if the oath relates to a document that is required or authorized to be filed in the office of the county tax assessor-collector;

(8) the secretary of state or a former secretary of state;

(9) an employee of a personal bond office, or an employee of a county, who is employed to obtain information required to be obtained under oath if the oath is required or authorized by Article 17.04 or by Article 26.04(n) or (o), Code of Criminal Procedure;

(10) the lieutenant governor or a former lieutenant governor;

(11) the speaker of the house of representatives or a former speaker of the house of representatives ;

(12) the governor or a former governor;

(13) a legislator or retired legislator;

(14) the attorney general or a former attorney general;

(15) the secretary or clerk of a municipality in a matter pertaining to the official business of the municipality; or

(16) a peace officer described by Article 2.12, Code of Criminal

Procedure, if: (A) the oath is administered when the officer is engaged in the performance of the officer's duties; and (B) the administration of the oath relates to the officer's duties.

Title 6. Public Officers and Employees
Subtitle A. Provisions Generally Applicable to Public Officer and Employees
Chapter 603. Provisions of Documents and Fees of Office

Sec. 603.001. Definition
Sec. 603.006. Fee Book
Sec. 603.007. Bill for Fees
Sec. 603.008. Posting of Fees Required
Sec. 603.010. Overcharging of Fees; Penalty

Sec. 603.001. Definition. In this chapter, "document" includes any instrument, paper, or other record. (1993, ch. 268, sec. 1)

Sec. 603.006. Fee Book. An officer who by law may charge a fee for a service shall keep a fee book and shall enter in the book all fees charged for services rendered. (1993, ch. 268, sec. 1; Formerly T.R.C.S., Article 3907)

Sec. 603.007. Bill for Fees. A fee under this chapter is not payable to a person until a clerk or officer produces, or is ready to produce, a bill in writing containing the details of the fee to the person who owes the fee. The bill must be signed by the clerk or officer to whom the fee is due or who charges the fee or by the successor in office or legal representative of the clerk or officer. (1993, ch. 268, sec. 1; Formerly T.R.C.S., Article 3908)

Sec. 603.008. Posting of Fees Required. A county judge, clerk of a district or county court, sheriff, justice of the peace, constable, or notary public shall keep posted at all times in a conspicuous place in the respective offices a complete list of fees the person may charge by law. (1993, ch. 268, sec. 1; Formerly T.R.C.S., Article 3910)

Sec. 603.010. Overcharging of Fees; Penalty. An officer named in this chapter who demands and receives a higher fee than authorized under this chapter or a fee that is not authorized under this chapter is liable to the aggrieved person for four times the amount unlawfully demanded and received. (1993, ch. 268, sec. 1; Formerly T.R.C.S., Article 3909)

TEXAS ADMINISTRATIVE CODE
TITLE 1. ADMINISTRATION
PART 4. OFFICE OF THE SECRETARY OF STATE
CHAPTER 87. NOTARY PUBLIC

SUBCHAPTER A. NOTARY PUBLIC QUALIFICATIONS

RULE §87.1. Application for a Commission as a Notary Public
(a) All persons applying for a commission as a notary public shall use the application form prescribed by the secretary of state.
(b) The application form may be obtained by writing the Office of the Secretary of State, Notary Public Unit, P.O. Box 12079, Austin, Texas 78711.
Source Note: The provisions of this §87.1 adopted to be effective September 7, 1988, 13 TexReg 4233; amended to be effective February 27,

1996, 21 TexReg 1269.

RULE §87.4. Issuance of the Notary Public Commission by the Secretary of State

(a) The secretary of state shall commission each applicant if:

(1) the application is properly completed and executed;

(2) the applicant is a resident of the United States and of Texas, and is at least 18 years of age;

(3) the applicant is eligible and no good cause is known for rejection of the application as provided by law and hereafter by §87.41 of this title (relating to Rejection of Application and Revocation of Commission);

(4) the fees specified in the Texas Government Code, §406.007, are submitted with the application form; and

(5) If a renewal, the form is received by the secretary of state no later than the expiration date of the term for which the notary public is presently serving.

(b) The secretary of state shall not commission an applicant if he or she has had a prior application rejected or a commission revoked for a finding of ineligibility or good cause which still continues.

(c) If any application is received that is not properly completed and executed, the qualification of that particular applicant will be delayed. The secretary of state shall notify the applicant by means of a rejection notice stating why the commission was not issued, and the steps which should be taken to correct the errors or omissions. The applicant will have 30 days from the date of the notice to respond; otherwise, the application will be considered abandoned and all fees deposited forfeited.

(d) When an applicant states that he or she has been convicted of either a felony or a crime involving moral turpitude, or for the violation of any law concerning the regulation of the conduct of notaries public, the secretary of state may request such additional facts or supporting documentation as may be deemed necessary for fair consideration of the application. Once a request for additional facts or supporting documentation is made, the applicant shall have 30 days from the date of the request to respond; otherwise, the application will be considered abandoned and all fees deposited forfeited.

Source Note: The provisions of this §87.4 adopted to be effective March 28, 1980, 5 TexReg 968; amended to be effective October 25, 1984, 9 TexReg 5269; amended to be effective October 7, 1992, 17 TexReg 6547; amended to be effective February 27, 1996, 21 TexReg 1269

RULE §87.22. Completion and Execution of the Bond and Statement of Officer

(a) The bond and statement of officer will be completed as follows.

(1) All information entered on the application will be legible.

(2) The name and social security number of the applicant will be entered in the space provided in the application.

(3) The complete name of the insurance or bonding company will be entered in the spaces provided in the bond.

(4) The name and address of the agent or agency will be entered in the space provided in the bond.

(5) The applicant will sign in the space provided for signature for

the principal. The surety officer or an attorney-in-fact for an insurance or bonding company will sign in the space provided and give the surety company's Texas Department of Insurance license number.

(6) A bond form that is preprinted with a surety company's name may be used only by that surety for the issuance of a notary bond.

(7) The applicant's name to be used as a notary public will be entered in the space provided in the statement of officer.

(8) The applicant will execute the statement of officer by signing in the space provided for signature. Both the initial qualification as well as renewals require the referenced statement of officer.

(b) An applicant who is an officer or employee of a state agency is not required to complete the surety bond. Such applicants will follow the procedure described in §87.25 of this Chapter.

(c) In this Chapter, "state agency" has the meaning assigned by Section 2052.101 of the Government Code.

Source Note: The provisions of this §87.22 adopted to be effective March 20, 1980, 5 TexReg 968; amended to be effective October 7, 1992, 17 TexReg 6547; amended to be effective February 27, 1996, 21 TexReg 1269; amended to be effective September 1, 2002, 27 TexReg 7787; amended to be effective December 11, 2003, 28 TexReg 10907

RULE §87.23. Review of the Bond and Statement of Officer

(a) The bond and statement of officer shall be approved by the secretary of state if:

(1) the form is properly completed and executed as hereinabove provided in §87.22(a) of this title (relating to Completion and Execution of the Bond and Statement of Officer); and

(2) the fees specified in the Notary Public Act, §406.007, Texas Government Code Annotated, §§406.001-406.024 (Vernon 1990) are remitted with the form to the secretary of state.

(b) When all conditions for qualification have been met, the application form shall be approved, stamped "qualified" with the date of qualification, and filed. The secretary of state shall cause a commission to be issued and sent to each notary public who has qualified, which commission shall be effective as of the date of qualification for a term of office as provided by law.

Source Note: The provisions of this §87.23 adopted to be effective March 28, 1980, 5 TexReg 968; amended to be effective October 25, 1984, 9 TexReg 5269; amended to be effective October 7, 1992, 17 TexReg 6547; amended to be effective February 27, 1996, 21 TexReg 1269.

RULE §87.25. Qualification by an Officer or Employee of a State Agency who does not furnish a Notary Public Bond

(a) Application for Appointment

(1) The applicant will complete the notary public application entitled: "Application for Appointment as a Notary Public Without Bond."

(2) The State Agency that employs the applicant will submit the completed application to the State Office of Risk Management for verification by that Office.

(3) The State Office of Risk Management will complete the verification certificate on the application, and forward the completed application to the Office of the Secretary of State for processing.

(b) Change in employment status.

(1) If a notary public transfers to another state agency, the notary public's new agency shall notify the State Office of Risk Management and the Office of the Secretary of State of the transfer.

(2) If a notary public terminates state employment, the notary public shall:

(A) voluntarily surrender the notary public commission;

(B) purchase a notary public bond for the time-period remaining on the notary's current term of office; or

(C) apply for a new term of office and provide a notary public bond.

Source Note: The provisions of this §87.25 adopted to be effective September 1, 2002, 27 TexReg 7787

SUBCHAPTER B. REJECTION AND REVOCATION

RULE §87.41. Rejection of Application and Revocation of Commission

The secretary of state by final decision and order may, for ineligibility or good cause, reject any application, suspend or revoke the commission of any notary public, or take other disciplinary action against a notary public. The other disciplinary action shall include, but not be limited to, those actions outlined in §87.48 of this title (relating to Other Disciplinary Acts). Rejection, revocation, and disciplinary proceedings will be held pursuant to the right of notice, hearing, and adjudication as set out in the rules of practice and procedure before the Office of the Secretary of State and the Administrative Procedure Act, Texas Government Code, §§2001.001-2001.902. Any party to a contested case has the right to be represented by legal counsel. Such action will be subject to the right of appeal to a district court of Travis County.

Source Note: The provisions of this §87.41 adopted to be effective March 20, 1980, 5 TexReg 968; amended to be effective February 25, 1988, 13 TexReg 778; amended to be effective February 27, 1996, 21 TexReg 1269.

RULE §87.42. Eligibility for Appointment or To Hold the Office of Notary Public

An application for appointment will be rejected if the applicant is not 18 years of age and a resident of the United States and Texas. A notary public commission will be revoked if the applicant was not at least 18 years of age at the time of appointment, or is no longer a resident of the United States and Texas. An applicant or notary public will no longer be eligible to hold the public office of notary public if convicted of a felony which has become final, and not set aside, for which no pardon or certificate of restoration of citizenship rights has been granted. The dismissal and discharge of proceedings under the adult probation, parole, and mandatory supervision law will not be considered a conviction for the purpose of determining a person's eligibility to be appointed or hold the office of notary public.

Source Note: The provisions of this §87.42 adopted to be effective March 28, 1980, 5 TexReg 968; amended to be effective October 25, 1984, 9 TexReg 5269.

RULE §87.43. Good Cause

(a) Good cause as stated in §87.41 of this title (relating to Rejection of Application and Revocation of Commission) may include, but not be limited to, the following:

(1) a final conviction for a crime involving moral turpitude;

(2) any false statement knowingly made in an application for appointment or reappointment as a notary public;

(3) a final conviction for the violation of any law concerning the regulation of the conduct of notaries public in this state or any other state;

(4) use of the phrase "notario" or "notario publico" to advertise the services of a notary public or any other false representation as an attorney as specified in the Texas Government Code, §406.017.

(5) a failure to fully and faithfully discharge any of the duties or responsibilities required of a notary public;

(6) the unauthorized practice of law;

(7) a failure by the notary public to utilize a correct notary seal as described in the Notary Public Act, §406.013;

(8) a failure to administer an oath or affirmation as required by law;

(9) the collection of a fee in excess of those authorized by the Texas Government Code, §406.024;

(10) the execution of any certificate as a notary public containing a statement known to the notary public to be false;

(11) a failure to complete the acknowledgment at the time the notary public's signature and seal are affixed to the document;

(12) the advertising in any manner whatsoever that the notary public is an immigration specialist, immigration consultant, or any other title or description reflecting an expertise in immigration matters;

(13) the use of false or misleading advertising of either an oral or written nature, whereby the notary public has represented or indicated that he or she has duties, rights, powers, or privileges that are not possessed by law;

(14) taking an acknowledgment when the person whose signature is acknowledged did not personally appear before the notary at the time of taking the acknowledgment;

(15) previous disciplinary action against the notary public in accordance with these sections; and

(16) a failure to comply with, or violation of, a previous disciplinary action taken pursuant to §87.48 of this title (relating to Other Disciplinary Action).

(b) A crime involving moral turpitude means the commission of a crime mala in se (an offense that is evil or wrong from its own nature or by natural law irrespective of statute) which may include, but not be limited to:

(1) Class A and B type misdemeanors; and

(2) felony convictions which have not been set aside, or for which no pardon or certificate of restoration of citizenship rights have been granted.

(c) The dismissal and discharge of proceedings under either the misdemeanor adult probation and supervision law or the adult probation, parole, and mandatory supervision law shall not be considered a conviction for the purposes of determining good cause.

(d) Final Class C type misdemeanor convictions shall not be considered in determining good cause.

Source Note: The provisions of this §87.43 adopted to be effective January 1, 1976; amended to be effective January 26, 1981, 6 TexReg 153; amended to be effective February 25, 1988, 13 TexReg 778; amended to be effective October 7, 1992, 17 TexReg 6547; amended to be effective October 18, 2001, 26 TexReg 8019

SUBCHAPTER C. ADMINISTRATIVE ACTION

RULE §87.44. Qualification under New Name

(a) During the four-year term of office, a notary public may change the name on the notary commission by submitting the following to the secretary of state:

(1) a completed change of name form;

(2) a rider or endorsement to the bond on file with the secretary of state from the surety company or its agent or representative specifying the change of name;

(3) the current certificate of commission or a statement that the notary public will perform all future notarial acts under the name specified on the amended commission; and

(4) the statutory fees for the issuance of a commission and the filing of a bond.

(b) The change of name will be effective as of the date of receipt of the properly completed and executed elements listed in this section.

(c) When the name change is effective, the notary public will perform all notarial acts using the name on the amended commission.

Source Note: The provisions of this §87.44 adopted to be effective November 10, 1986, 11 TexReg 4482; amended to be effective February 27, 1996, 21 TexReg 1269.

RULE §87.45. Rejection

If the submission of the change of name does not comply with §87.44(a) of this title (relating to Qualification under New Name), the secretary of state shall notify the notary public in writing of any deficiency. The notary public shall have 30 days from the date of the notice to respond; if no response is received, the request for the change of name will be considered abandoned and all fees paid will be forfeited.

Source Note: The provisions of this §87.45 adopted to be effective November 10, 1986, 11 TexReg 4482.

RULE §87.46. Issuance of Amended Commission

The secretary of state shall issue an amended commission to the notary public in the name requested.

Source Note: The provisions of this §87.46 adopted to be effective November 10, 1986, 11 TexReg 4482.

RULE §87.47. Complaint Procedures

(a) A person harmed by the actions of a notary public may file a complaint with the secretary of state. The complaint shall be filed on the form prescribed by the secretary of state for such purposes, shall be signed and verified by the person alleging misconduct on the part of the notary public, and shall substantially comply with the requirements set forth on the prescribed form.

(b) The complaint shall be reviewed by an employee of the secretary of state to determine if the complaint substantially complies with the requirements set forth on the prescribed form and if the actions complained of are sufficient to constitute good cause for suspension, revocation, or other disciplinary action.

(c) The secretary of state may determine that the actions of the notary public are not sufficiently egregious to warrant formal disciplinary action. The secretary may determine to take no action on the complaint, or the secretary may determine to informally advise the notary public of the appropriate conduct and the applicable statutes and rules governing the conduct. The secretary of state shall notify the complainant of the determination not to take further or formal action.

(d) If the secretary of state determines that the complaint alleges sufficient facts to constitute good cause for the suspension or revocation of the notary public's commission, or other disciplinary action against the notary public, the secretary of state shall notify the notary public of the filing of the complaint and send a copy of the complaint to the notary public.

(e) If the secretary of state determines to proceed on a complaint, the notary public shall be required to respond to the complaint within 20 days of mailing of the notice of complaint to the notary public. The response shall be in writing; the response should specify any disputed facts and provide such additional information as the notary public shall desire.

(f) The secretary of state shall review the response, and determine whether further administrative action is appropriate. If the secretary determines that no further action is appropriate, the secretary shall notify in writing the notary public and the complainant of the determination.

(g) If the secretary determines that further administrative action is appropriate, the secretary shall cause the initiation of a contested case under the rules of practice and procedure before the Office of the Secretary of State.

Source Note: The provisions of this §87.47 adopted to be effective February 25, 1988, 13 TexReg 778.

RULE §87.48. Other Disciplinary Action

(a) The secretary of state may determine that the conduct which is the basis of a complaint against a notary public does not warrant the suspension or revocation of the commission of the notary public. In the discretion of the secretary of state and after the initiation of a contested case, the secretary of state may seek, but is not limited to, the following disciplinary actions:

(1) official reprimand to the public notary;

(2) a consent decree to cease and desist from engaging from any further misconduct;

(3) an agreement to voluntarily surrender the notary public commission;

(4) an agreement to complete a course of study relating to the powers, duties, and responsibilities of a notary public;

(5) an agreement not to seek renewal of a notary public commission for a specified period of time; or

(6) to take such information action as the secretary deems appropriate.

(b) If no agreement can be reached, the secretary of state shall give written notice to the affected party of a right to a hearing in accordance with the rules of practice and procedure before the secretary of state.

Source Note: The provisions of this §87.48 adopted to be effective February 25, 1988, 13 TexReg 778; amended to be effective October 7, 1992, 17 TexReg 6547.

RULE §87.49. Time for Action

(a) A complaint which arises during the time of office of a notary public which is not disposed of prior to the end of the term may be pursued in a subsequent term of office. The secretary of state shall not be barred from seeking suspension or revocation of a notary public for acts or omission which occurred during a prior term of office.

(b) In the discretion of the secretary of state, the secretary may determine to take other disciplinary action after the expiration of the term of office of a notary public regardless of whether the notary public has renewed or will seek to renew the notary public commission.

Source Note: The provisions of this §87.49 adopted to be effective February 25, 1988, 13 TexReg 778

SUBCHAPTER D. SUBPOENAS

RULE §87.50. Authority

A notary public is authorized to issue a subpoena or subpoena duces tecum for written depositions. This is a powerful authorization and should be exercised cautiously.

Source Note: The provisions of this §87.50 adopted to be effective June 2, 1993, 18 TexReg 3277.

RULE §87.52. Issuing

Prior to issuing a subpoena, the notary shall:

(1) require proof of service of notice to take a deposition from the requesting party or attorney; or

(2) personally execute service of the notice to take a deposition. Additionally, the notary shall confirm that there is no court or administrative order or procedure that precludes the issuance of the subpoena. The notary shall obtain an affidavit from the requesting party or attorney stating whether the party or attorney is aware of any such procedure or order.

Source Note: The provisions of this §87.52 adopted to be effective June 2, 1993, 18 TexReg 3277.

RULE §87.54. Governed by Other Law

These rules do not independently authorize a notary public to issue a subpoena. The issuance of a subpoena by a notary public must be authorized by other law, rule, or procedure and in conformity with such law, rule, or procedure. Failure of a notary public to conform to these administrative rules does not affect the validity of a subpoena but may subject the notary public to disciplinary proceedings by the Office of the Secretary of State.

Source Note: The provisions of this §87.54 adopted to be effective June 2, 1993, 18 TexReg 3277.

SUBCHAPTER E. NOTARY RECORDS

RULE §87.60. Prohibition Against Recording Personal Information

(a) A notary public (other than a court clerk notarizing instruments for the court) that notarizes a document or instrument on behalf of a signer, grantor or maker that is identified to the notary by an identification card issued by a governmental agency or a passport issued by the United States may not record in the notary's book of record:

(1) the identification number that was assigned by the governmental agency or by the United States to the signer, grantor or maker and that is set forth on the identification card or passport; or

(2) any other number that could be used to identify the signer, grantor or maker of the document.

(b) Nothing in this section shall be construed to prohibit a notary from recording a number related to the residence or alleged residence of the signer, grantor or maker of the document or the instrument.

Source Note: The provisions of this §87.60 adopted to be effective April 22, 2007, 32 TexReg 2275

Texas Civil Practice and Remedies Code
Title 6. Miscellaneous Provisions
Chapter 121. Acknowledgments and Proofs of Written Instruments

Sec. 121.001. Officers Who May Take Acknowledgments and Proofs
Sec. 121.002. Corporate Acknowledgments
Sec. 121.003. Authority of Officers
Sec. 121.004. Method of Acknowledgment
Sec. 121.005. Proof of Identity of Acknowledging Person
Sec. 121.006. Alteration of Authorized Forms; Definition.
Sec. 121.007. Form for Ordinary Certificate of Acknowledgment
Sec. 121.008. Short Forms for Certificates of Acknowledgment
Sec. 121.009. Proof of Acknowledgment by Witness
Sec. 121.010. Form of Certificate for Proof by Witness
Sec. 121.011. Proof of Acknowledgment by Handwriting
Sec. 121.012. Record of Acknowledgment
Sec. 121.013. Subpoena of Witness; Attachment
Sec. 121.014. Action for Damages

Sec. 121.001. Officers Who May Take Acknowledgments and Proofs. (a) An acknowledgment or proof of a written instrument may be taken in this state by:

(1) a clerk of a district court;

(2) a judge or clerk of a county court; or

(3) a notary public; or

(4) a county tax assessor-collector or an employee of the county tax assessor-collector if the instrument is required or authorized to be filed in the office of the county tax assessor-collector.

(b) An acknowledgment or proof of a written instrument may be taken outside this state, but inside the United States or its territories, by:

(1) a clerk of a court of record having a seal;

(2) a commissioner of deeds appointed under the laws of this state; or

(3) a notary public.

(c) An acknowledgment or proof of a written instrument may be taken outside the United States and its territories by:

(1) A minister, commissioner, or charge d'affaires of the United States who is a resident of and is accredited in the country where the acknowledgment or proof is taken;

(2) a consul-general, consul, vice-consul, commercial agent, vice-commercial agent, deputy consul, or consular agent of the United States who is a resident of the country where the acknowledgment or proof is taken; or

(3) a notary public or any other official authorized to administer oaths in the jurisdiction where the acknowledgment or proof is taken.

(d) A commissioned officer of the United States Armed Forces or of a United States Armed Forces Auxiliary may take acknowledgment or proof of a written instrument of a member of the armed forces, a member of an armed forces auxiliary, or a member's spouse. If an acknowledgment or proof is taken under this subsection, it is presumed, absent pleading and proof to the contrary, that the commissioned officer who signed was a commissioned officer on the date that the officer signed, and that the acknowledging person was a member of the authorized group of military personnel or spouses. The failure of the commissioned officer to attach an official seal to the certificate of acknowledgment or proof of an instrument does not invalidate the acknowledgment or proof. (1985, ch. 959, sec. 1; 1987, ch. 891, sec. 1; 1995, ch. 165, sec. 18)

Sec. 121.002. Corporate Acknowledgments. (a) An employee of a corporation is not disqualified because of his employment from taking an acknowledgment or proof of a written instrument in which the corporation has an interest.

(b) An Officer who is a shareholder in a corporation is not disqualified from taking an acknowledgment or proof of an instrument in which the corporation has an interest unless: (1) the corporation has 1,000 or fewer shareholders; and (2) the officer owns more than one-tenth of one percent of the issued and outstanding stock. (1985, ch. 959, sec. 1)

Sec 121.003. Authority of Officers. In a proceeding to prove a written instrument, an officer authorized by this chapter to take an acknowledgment or proof of a written instrument is also authorized to:

(1) administer oaths;

(2) employ and swear interpreters; and

(3) issue subpoenas. (1985, ch. 959, sec. 1)

Sec. 121.004. Method of Acknowledgment. (a) To acknowledge a written instrument for recording, the grantor or person who executed the instrument must appear before an officer and must state that he executed the instrument for the purposes and consideration expressed in it.

(b) The officer shall:

(1) make a certificate of acknowledgment;

(2) sign the certificate; and

(3) seal the certificate with the seal of office.

(c) The failure of a notary public to attach an official seal to a certificate of an acknowledgment or proof of a written instrument made outside this state but inside the United States or its territories renders the acknowledgment or proof invalid only if the jurisdiction in which the

107

certificate is made required the notary public to attach the seal. (1985, ch. 959, sec. 1; 1995, ch. 603, sec. 1)

(d) The application of an embossed seal is not required on an electronically transmitted certificate of acknowledgment. (1985, ch. 959, sec. 1; 1995, ch. 603, sec. 1; 2001, ch. 95, sec. 1)

Sec. 121.005. Proof of Identity of Acknowledging Person. (a) An officer may not take the acknowledgment of a written instrument unless the officer knows or has satisfactory evidence that the acknowledging person is the person who executed the instrument and is described in it. An officer may accept, as satisfactory evidence of the identity of an acknowledging person, only:

(1) the oath of a credible witness personally known to the officer; or

(2) a current identification card or other document issued by the federal government or any state government that contains the photograph and signature of the acknowledging person.

(3) with respect to a deed or other instrument relating to a residential real estate transaction, a current passport issued by a foreign country.

(b) Except in a short form certificate of acknowledgment authorized by Section 121.008, the officer must note in the certificate of acknowledgment that:

(1) he personally knows the acknowledging person; or

(2) evidence of a witness or an identification card or other document was used to identify the acknowledging person. (1985, ch. 959, sec. 1; 1997, ch. 90, sec. 1)

Sec. 121.006. Alteration of Authorized Forms; Definition. (a) An acknowledgment form provided by this chapter may be altered as circumstances require. The authorization of a form does not prevent the use of other forms. The marital status or other status of the acknowledging person may be shown after the person's name..

(b) In acknowledgment form "acknowledged" means:

(1) in the case of a natural person, that the person personally appeared before the officer taking the acknowledgment and acknowledged executing the instrument for the purposes and consideration expressed in it;

(2) in the case of a person as principal by an attorney-in-fact for the principal, that the attorney-in-fact personally appeared before the officer taking the acknowledgment and that the attorney-in-fact acknowledged executing the instrument as the act of the principal for the purposes and consideration expressed in it;

(3) in the case of a partnership by a partner or partners acting for the partnership, that the partner or partners personally appeared before the officer taking the acknowledgment and acknowledged executing the instrument as the act of the partnership for the purposes and consideration expressed in it;

(4) in the case of a corporation by a corporate officer or agent, that the corporate officer or agent personally appeared before the officer taking the acknowledgment and that the corporate officer of agent acknowledged executing the instrument in the capacity stated, as the act of the corporation, for the purposes and consideration expressed in it; and

(5) in the case of a person acknowledging as a public officer, trustee,

executor or administrator of an estate, guardian, or other representative, that the person personally appeared before the officer taking the acknowledgment and acknowledged executing the instrument by proper authority in the capacity stated and for the purposes and consideration expressed in it. (1985, ch. 959, sec. 1)

Sec. 121.007. Form for Ordinary Certificate of Acknowledgment. The form of an ordinary certificate of acknowledgment must be substantially as follows:

The State of _____,
County of _____,

Before me _____ (here insert the name and character of the officer) on this day personally appeared _____, known to me (or proved to me on the oath of _____ or through _____ (description of identity card or other document)) to be the person whose name is subscribed to the foregoing instrument and acknowledged to me that he executed the same for the purposes and consideration therein expressed.
(Seal) "Given under my hand and seal of office this _____ day of _____, A.D., _____.

(1985, ch. 959, sec. 1; 1997, ch. 90, sec. 1)

Sec. 121.008. Short Forms for Certificate of Acknowledgment. (a) The forms for certificates of acknowledgment provided by this section may be used as alternatives to other authorized forms. They may be referred to as "statutory forms of acknowledgment."

(b) Short forms for certificates of acknowledgment include:

(1) For a natural person acting in his own right.

State of _____
County of _____

This instrument was acknowledged before me on _____ (date) by _____ (name or names of person or persons acknowledging).

(Signature of officer)
(Title of officer)
My commission expires: _____

(2) For a natural person as principal acting by attorney-in-fact:

State of _____
County of _____
This instrument was acknowledged before me on _____ (date) by _____ (name of attorney-in-fact) as attorney-in-fact on behalf of _____ (name of principal).

(Signature of officer)
(Title of officer)
My commission expires: _____

(3) For a partnership acting by one or more partners:

State of _____

County of _____

This instrument was acknowledged before me on _____ (date) by _____ (name of acknowledging partner or partners), partner(s) on behalf of _____ (name of partnership), a partnership.

(Signature of officer)

(Title of officer)

My commission expires: _____

(4) For a corporation:

State of _____

County of _____

This instrument was acknowledged before me on _____ (date) by _____ (name of officer), (title of officer) of (name of corporation acknowledging) a _____ (state of incorporation) corporation, on behalf of said corporation.

(Signature of officer)

(Title of officer)

My commission expires: _____

(5) For a public officer, trustee, executor, administrator, guardian, or other representative:

State of _____

County of _____

This instrument was acknowledged before me on _____ (date) by_____ (name of representative) as _____ (title of representative) of _____ (name of entity or person represented).

(Signature of officer)

(Title of officer)

My commission expires: _____

(1985, ch. 959, sec. 1)

Sec. 121.009. Proof of Acknowledgment by Witness. (a) To prove a written instrument for recording, at least one of the witnesses who signed the instrument must personally appear before an officer who is authorized by this chapter to take acknowledgments or proofs and must swear:

(1) either that he saw the grantor or person who executed the instrument sign it or that that person acknowledged in the presence of the witness that he executed the instrument for the purposes and consideration expressed in it; and

(2) that he signed the instrument at the request of the grantor or person who executed the instrument.

(b) The officer must make a certificate of the testimony of the witness and must sign and officially seal the certificate.

(c) The officer may take the testimony of a witness only if the officer personally knows or has satisfactory evidence on the oath of a credible witness that the individual testifying is the person who signed the instrument as a witness that the individual testifying is the person who signed the instrument as a witness. If evidence is used to identify the witness who signed the instrument, the officer must note the use of the evidence in the certificate of acknowledgment. (1985, ch. 959, sec. 1)

Sec. 121.010. Form of Certificate for Proof by Witness. When the execution of a written instrument is proved by a witness, the certificate of the officer must be substantially as follows:

The State of _____,
County of _____,

Before me, _____ (here insert the name and character of the officer), on this day personally appeared _____, known to me (or proved to me on the oath of _____), to be the person whose name is subscribed as a witness to the foregoing instrument of writing, and after being duly sworn by me stated on oath that he saw_____, the grantor or person who executed the foregoing instrument, subscribe the same (or that the grantor or person who executed such instrument of writing acknowledged in his presence that he had executed the same for the purposes and consideration therein expressed), and that he had signed the same as a witness at the request of the grantor (or person who executed the same).
(Seal) "Given under my hand and seal of office this _____ day of _____, A.D., _____.

(1985, ch. 959, sec. 1)

Sec. 121.011. Proof of Acknowledgment by Handwriting. (a) The execution of an instrument may be established for recording by proof of the handwriting of persons who signed the instrument only if:

(1) the grantor of the instrument and all of the witnesses are dead;

(2) the grantor and all of the witnesses are not residents of this state;

(3) the residences of the grantor and the witnesses are unknown to the person seeking to prove the instrument and cannot be ascertained;

(4) the witnesses have become legally incompetent to testify; or

(5) the grantor of the instrument refuses to acknowledge the execution of the instrument and all of the witnesses are dead, not residents of this state, or legally incompetent or their places of residence are unknown.

(b) If the grantor or person who executed the instrument signed his name to the instrument, its execution must be proved by evidence of the handwriting of that person and at least one witness who signed the instrument. If the grantor or person who executed the instrument signed the instrument by making his mark, its execution must be proved by the handwriting of at least two of the witnesses who signed the instrument.

(c) Evidence taken for proof of handwriting must give the residence of the testifying witness. A testifying witness must have known the person whose handwriting is being proved and must be well acquainted with the handwriting in question and recognize it as genuine.

(d) Evidence offered for proof of handwriting must be given in writing by the deposition or affidavit of two or more disinterested persons. The evidence must satisfactorily prove to the officer each of the requirements provided by this section. The officer taking the proof must certify the witnesses' testimony. The officer must sign, officially seal, and attach this certificate to the instrument with the depositions or affidavits of the witnesses. (1985, ch. 959, sec. 1)

Sec. 121.012. Record of Acknowledgment. (a) An officer authorized by law to take an acknowledgment or proof of a written instrument required or permitted by law to be recorded must enter in a well-bound book and officially sign a short statement of each acknowledgment or proof. The statement must contain the date that the acknowledgment or proof was taken, the date of the instrument, and the names of the grantor and grantee of the instrument.

(b) If the execution of the instrument is acknowledged by the grantor of the instrument, the statement must also contain:

(1) the grantor's known or alleged residence;

(2) whether the grantor is personally known to the officer; and

(3) if the grantor is unknown to the officer, the name and residence of the person who introduced the grantor to the officer, if any.

(c) If the execution of the instrument is proved by a witness who signed the instrument, the statement must also contain:

(1) the name of the witness;

(2) the known or alleged residence of the witness;

(3) whether the witness is personally known to the officer; and

(4) if the witness is unknown to the officer, the name and known or alleged residence of the person who introduced the witness to the officer, if any.

(d) If land is charged or conveyed by the instrument, the statement must also contain:

(1) the name of the original grantee; and

(2) the name of the county in which the land is located.

(e) The statements of acknowledgment recorded by the officer are original public records, open for public inspection and examination at all reasonable times. The officer must deliver the book to his successor in office. (1985, ch. 959, sec. 1)

Sec. 121.013. Subpoena of Witness; Attachment. (a) On the sworn application of a person interested in the proof of an instrument required or permitted by law to be recorded, stating that a witness to the instrument refuses to appear and testify regarding the execution of an instrument and that the instrument cannot be proven without the evidence of the witness, an officer authorized to take proofs of instruments shall issue a subpoena requiring the witness to appear before the officer and testify about the execution of the instrument.

(b) If the witness fails to obey the subpoena, the officer has the same powers to enforce the attendance and compel the answers of the witness as does a district judge. Attachment may not be issued, however, unless the witness receives or is tendered the same compensation that is made to witnesses in other cases. An officer may not require the witness to leave his county of residence, but if the witness is temporarily present in the county where the execution of the instrument is sought to be proven for registration, he may be required to appear. (1985, ch. 959, sec. 1)

Sec. 121.014. Action for Damages. A person injured by the failure, refusal, or neglect of an officer to comply with a provision of this chapter has a cause of action against the officer to recover damages resulting from the failure, refusal, or neglect of the officer. (1985, ch. 959, sec. 1)

Texas Health and Safety Code
Chapter 166. Advance Directives

Section 166.002.

(5-a) "Digital signature" means an electronic identifier intended by the person using it to have the same force and effect as the use of a manual signature.

(5-b) "Electronic signature" means a facsimile, scan, uploaded image, computer-generated image, or other electronic representation of a manual signature that is intended by the person using it to have the same force and effect of law as a manual signature.

Section 166.011. DIGITAL OR ELECTRONIC SIGNATURE. (a) For an advance directive in which a signature by a declarant, witness, or notary public is required or used, the declarant, witness, or notary public may sign the directive or a written revocation of the directive using:

(1) a digital signature that:

(A) uses an algorithm approved by the department;

(B) is unique to the person using it;

(C) is capable of verification;

(D) is under the sole control of the person using it;

(E) is linked to data in a manner that invalidates the digital signature if the data is changed;

(F) persists with the document and not by association in separate files; and

(G) is bound to a digital certificate; or

(2) an electronic signature that:

(A) is capable of verification;

(B) is under the sole control of the person using it;

(C) is linked to data in a manner that invalidates the electronic signature if the data is changed; and

(D) persists with the document and not by association in separate files.

(b) In approving an algorithm for purposes of Subsection (a)(1)(A), the department may consider an algorithm approved by the National Institute of Standards and Technology.

(c) The executive commissioner of the Health and Human Services Commission by rule shall modify the advance directive forms required under this chapter as necessary to provide for the use of a digital or electronic signature that complies with the requirements of this section.

Section 166.032
***

(b) Except as provided by Subsection (b-1), the The declarant must sign the directive in the presence of two witnesses who qualify under Section 166.003, at least one of whom must be a witness who qualifies under Section 166.003(2). The witnesses must sign the directive.

(b-1) The declarant, in lieu of signing in the presence of witnesses, may sign the directive and have the signature acknowledged before a notary public.

Section 166.036

(a) Except as provided by Section 166.032(b-1), a A written directive executed under Section 166.033 or 166.035 is effective without regard to whether the document has been notarized.

Section 166.082

***

(b) Except as provided by this subsection, the The declarant must sign the out-of-hospital DNR order in the presence of two witnesses who qualify under Section 166.003, at least one of whom must be a witness who qualifies under Section 166.003(2). The witnesses must sign the order. The attending physician of the declarant must sign the order and shall make the fact of the existence of the order and the reasons for execution of the order a part of the declarant's medical record. The declarant, in lieu of signing in the presence of witnesses, may sign the out-of-hospital DNR order and have the signature acknowledged before a notary public.

(c) If the person is incompetent but previously executed or issued a directive to physicians in accordance with Subchapter B, the physician may rely on the directive as the person's instructions to issue an out-of-hospital DNR order and shall place a copy of the directive in the person's medical record. The physician shall sign the order in lieu of the person signing under Subsection (b) and may use a digital or electronic signature authorized under Section 166.011 .

Section 166.083

***

(b) The standard form of an out-of-hospital DNR order specified by the board must, at a minimum, contain the following:

(1) a distinctive single-page format that readily identifies the document as an out-of-hospital DNR order;

(2) a title that readily identifies the document as an out-of-hospital DNR order;

(3) the printed or typed name of the person;

(4) a statement that the physician signing the document is the attending physician of the person and that the physician is directing health care professionals acting in out-of-hospital settings, including a hospital emergency department, not to initiate or continue certain life-sustaining treatment on behalf of the person, and a listing of those procedures not to be initiated or continued;

(5) a statement that the person understands that the person may revoke the out-of-hospital DNR order at any time by destroying the order and removing the DNR identification device, if any, or by communicating to health care professionals at the scene the person's desire to revoke the out-of-hospital DNR order;

(6) places for the printed names and signatures of the witnesses or the notary public's acknowledgment and for the printed name and signature of

the attending physician of the person and the medical license number of the attending physician;

(7) a separate section for execution of the document by the legal guardian of the person, the person's proxy, an agent of the person having a medical power of attorney, or the attending physician attesting to the issuance of an out-of-hospital DNR order by nonwritten means of communication or acting in accordance with a previously executed or previously issued directive to physicians under Section 166.082(c) that includes the following:

(A) a statement that the legal guardian, the proxy, the agent, the person by nonwritten means of communication, or the physician directs that each listed life-sustaining treatment should not be initiated or continued in behalf of the person; and

(B) places for the printed names and signatures of the witnesses and, as applicable, the legal guardian, proxy, agent, or physician;

(8) a separate section for execution of the document by at least one qualified relative of the person when the person does not have a legal guardian, proxy, or agent having a medical power of attorney and is incompetent or otherwise mentally or physically incapable of communication, including:

(A) a statement that the relative of the person is qualified to make a treatment decision to withhold cardiopulmonary resuscitation and certain other designated life-sustaining treatment under Section 166.088 and, based on the known desires of the person or a determination of the best interest of the person, directs that each listed life-sustaining treatment should not be initiated or continued in behalf of the person; and

(B) places for the printed names and signatures of the witnesses and qualified relative of the person;

(9) a place for entry of the date of execution of the document;

(10) a statement that the document is in effect on the date of its execution and remains in effect until the death of the person or until the document is revoked;

(11) a statement that the document must accompany the person during transport;

(12) a statement regarding the proper disposition of the document or copies of the document, as the board determines appropriate; and

(13) a statement at the bottom of the document, with places for the signature of each person executing the document, that the document has been properly completed.

Section 166.089
***

(d) The responding health care professionals must determine that the out-of-hospital DNR order form appears to be valid in that it includes:

(1) written responses in the places designated on the form for the names, signatures, and other information required of persons executing or issuing, or witnessing or acknowledging as applicable, the execution or issuance of, the order;

(2) a date in the place designated on the form for the date the order

115

was executed or issued; and

(3) the signature or digital or electronic signature of the declarant or persons executing or issuing the order and the attending physician in the appropriate places designated on the form for indicating that the order form has been properly completed.

Section 166.154 EXECUTION AND WITNESSES

(a) Except as provided by Subsection (b), the The medical power of attorney must be signed by the principal in the presence of two witnesses who qualify under Section 166.003, at least one of whom must be a witness who qualifies under Section 166.003(2). The witnesses must sign the document.

(b) The principal, in lieu of signing in the presence of the witnesses, may sign the medical power of attorney and have the signature acknowledged before a notary public.

(c) (b) If the principal is physically unable to sign, another person may sign the medical power of attorney with the principal's name in the principal's presence and at the principal's express direction. The person may use a digital or electronic signature authorized under Section 166.011.

SECTION 9. (a) Not later than December 1, 2009, the executive commissioner of the Health and Human Services Commission shall adopt the rules and modify the forms as necessary to comply with the changes in law made by this Act.

(b) Notwithstanding Chapter 166, Health and Safety Code, as amended by this Act, a person may not sign an advance directive or a written revocation of an advance directive using a digital or electronic signature before January 1, 2010.

Texas Business and Commerce Code

Sec. 322.011 Notarization and Acknowledgment

If a law requires a signature or record to be notarized, acknowledged, verified, or made under oath, the requirement is satisfied if the electronic signature of the person authorized to perform those acts, together with all other information required to be included by other applicable law, is attached to or logically associated with the signature or record.

Texas Insurance Code

Sec. 2652.051. LICENSE APPLICATION.
***

(c) The completed application must state that: (1) the proposed escrow officer is an individual who is a bona fide resident of: (A) this state; or (B) a state adjacent to this state ; (2) the proposed escrow officer is an attorney or is a bona fide employee of: (A) an attorney licensed as an escrow officer; or (B) a title insurance agent or direct operation; (3) the proposed escrow officer has reasonable experience or instruction in the field of title insurance; and (4) the title insurance agent or direct operation does not know of any fact or condition that disqualifies the proposed escrow officer from receiving a license ; and (5) the proposed escrow officer is a bona fide employee of a title insurance agent or direct operation with an office in this state . (d)

Notwithstanding Sections 406.004 and 406.020, Government Code, a person qualified under this section as an escrow officer may hold a license and operate as a notary public under Chapter 406, Government Code.

Sec. 2652.103. AMOUNT OF BOND OR DEPOSIT. (a) The amount of the bond or deposit required under this subchapter is determined by multiplying the number of escrow officers employed by the title insurance agent or direct operation by: (1) $5,000 for an application of an individual who is a bona fide resident of this state; or (2) $10,000 for an application of an individual who is a bona fide resident of a state adjacent to this state. (b) Notwithstanding Subsection (a), except that the maximum amount of the bond or deposit required under this subchapter is $50,000.

Sec. 2652.201. GROUNDS FOR LICENSE DENIAL OR DISCIPLINARY ACTION. (a) The department may deny an application for a license or discipline an escrow officer under Sections 4005.102, 4005.103, and 4005.104 if the department determines that the applicant or license holder has: (1) wilfully violated this title; (2) intentionally made a material misstatement in the license application; (3) obtained or attempted to obtain the license by fraud or misrepresentation; (4) misappropriated or converted to the escrow officer's own use or illegally withheld money belonging to a title insurance agent, direct operation, or another person; (5) been guilty of fraudulent or dishonest practices; (6) materially misrepresented the terms and conditions of a title insurance policy or contract; or (7) failed to complete all educational requirements. (b) The department may not deny an application for a license or discipline an escrow officer under Section 4005.102, 4005.103, or 4005.104 solely because the individual resides in an adjacent state and acts as an escrow officer in this state as a bona fide employee of a title insurance agent or direct operation in this state. SECTION 4. This Act applies to an application to act as an escrow officer that is filed with the Texas Department of Insurance on or after the effective date of this Act. An application filed before that date is governed by the law in effect on the date the application was filed, and the former law is continued in effect for that purpose.

Texas Property Code

Sec. 15.004. Validity of Electronic Documents.

(a) If a law requires, as a condition for recording, that a document be an original, be on paper or another tangible medium, or be in writing, the requirement is satisfied by an electronic document that complies with the requirements of this chapter.

(b) If a law requires, as a condition for recording, that a document be signed, the requirement is satisfied by an electronic signature.

(c) A requirement that a document or a signature associated with a document be notarized, acknowledged, verified, witnessed, or made under oath is satisfied if the electronic signature of the person authorized to perform that act, and all other information required to be included, is attached to or logically associated with the document or signature. A physical or electronic image of a stamp, impression, or seal need not accompany an electronic signature. ■

Office
of the Texas
Secretary of State

Secretary of State
Notary Public Unit

Street Address (also used for courier mail):
        Secretary of State
        Notary Public Unit
        1019 Brazos, #214
        Austin, TX 78701

Mailing Address:
        Secretary of State
        Notary Public Unit
        P.O. Box 13375
        Austin, TX 78711-3375

Telephone: (512) 463-5705

In addition, there are many useful resources available at the state's official Web site, including links to legislation, the Secretary of State's office and research bureaus. You can access the state's home page at www.state.tx.us.

You can also access the Secretary of State's office directly at www.sos.state.tx.us. Information for Notaries appears under the "Functions of Office" heading. ■

County Court Administrators' Offices

Many notarized documents — particularly deeds and mortgage documents — are publicly recorded at the local office of the County Clerk/Recorder. The addresses of these offices are listed below.

This list can be of additional use to those needing access to, or authenticated copies of, Notary records left in the custody of county clerks who have been appointed deputy custodians of notarial records. (See TGC, Section 406.023.)

Anderson County
500 N. Church
Street, #10
Palestine 75801
(903) 723-7432

Andrews County
P.O. Box 727
Andrews 79714
(432) 524-1426

Angelina County
P.O. Box 908
Lufkin 75902
(936) 634-8339

Arkansas County
301 N. Live Oak
Street
Rockport 78382
(361) 790-0122

Archer County
P.O. Box 427
Archer City 76351
(940) 574-4302

Armstrong County
P.O. Box 309
Claude 79019
(806) 226-2081

Atascosa County
#1 Courthouse
Circle, Ste. 102
Jourdanton 78026
(830) 767-2511

Austin County
One East Main
Bellville 77418
(979) 865-5911

Bailey County
300 South First St.
Ste. 200
Muleshoe 79347
(806) 272-3044

Bandera County
P.O. Box 823
Bandera 78003
(830) 796-3332

Bastrop County
P.O. Box 577
Bastrop 78602
(512) 332-7234

Baylor County
101 S. Washington
Seymour 76380
(940) 889-3322

Bee County
105 W. Corpus
Christi St., Rm. #108
Beeville 78102
(361) 362-3245

Bell County
P.O. Box 480
Belton 76513
(254) 933-5160

Bexar County
100 Dolorosa
Ste. 104
San Antonio 78205
(210) 335-2216

Blanco County
P.O. Box 65
Johnson City 78636
(830) 868-7357

Borden County
P.O. Box 124
Gail 79738
(806) 756-4312

Bosque County
P.O. Box 617
Meridian 76665
(254) 435-2201

Bowie County
P.O. Box 248
New Boston 75570
(903) 628-6742

Brazoria County
111 E. Locust
Ste 200
Angleton 77515
(979) 864-1355

Brazos County
300 E. 26th St.
Ste. 120
Bryan 77803
(979) 361-4135

Brewster County
P.O. Box 119
Alpine 79831
(432) 837-3366

Briscoe County
P.O. Box 555
Silverton 79257
(806) 823-2134

Brooks County
P.O. Box 427
Falfurrias 78355
(361) 325-5604

Brown County
200 South
Broadway
Brownwood 76801
(325) 643-2594

Burleson County
100 West Buck
Street, Suite 203
Caldwell 77836
(979) 567-2329

Burnet County
220 South Pierce St.
Burnet 78611
(512) 756-5406

Caldwell County
P.O. Box 906
Lockhart 78644
(512) 398-1804

Calhoun County
211 S. Ann St.
Port Lavaca 77979
(361) 553-4411

Callahan County
100 W. 4th St.
Suite 104
Baird 79504
(325) 854-5815

Cameron County
P.O. Box 2178
Brownsville 78520
(956) 544-0815

Camp County
126 Church Street
Pittsburg 75686
(903) 856-2731

Carson County
P.O. Box 487
Panhandle 79068
(806) 537-3873

Cass County
P.O. Box 449
Linden 75563
(903) 756-5071

Castro County
100 East Bedford
Room 101
Dimmitt 79027
(806) 647-3338

Chambers County
P.O. Box 728
Anahuac 77514
(409) 267-8309

Cherokee County
P.O. Box 420
Rusk 75785
(903) 683-2350

Childress County
Courthouse, Box 4
Childress 79201
(940) 937-6143

Clay County
100 North Bridge
Henrietta 76365
(940) 538-4631

Cochran County
100 N. Main
Room 102
Morton 79346
(806) 266-5450

Coke County
13 E. 7th Street
Robert Lee 76945
(325) 453-2631

Coleman County
100 West Liveoak,
Ste 105
Coleman 76834
(325) 625-2889

Collin County
200 S. McDonald
St., Annex A
Ste 120
McKinney 75069
(972) 548-4139

**Collingsworth
County**
Courthouse
800 W. Ave., Box 10
Wellington 79095
(806) 447-2408

Colorado County
400 Spring Street
Suite 103
Columbus 78934
(979) 732-6561

Comal County
150 N. Seguin Ave.
Ste. 101
New Braunfels
78130
(830) 221-1230

Comanche County
101 West Central
Comanche 76442
(325) 356-2655

Concho County
P.O. Box 98
Paint Rock 76866
(325) 732-4322

Cooke County
100 S. Dixon
Gainesville 76240
(940) 668-5420

Coryell County
P.O. Box 237
Gatesville 76528
(254) 865-5911

Cottle County
P.O. Box 717
Paducah 79248
(806) 492-3823

Crane County
P.O. Box 578
Crane 79731
(432) 558-3581

Crockett County
P.O. Drawer C
Ozona 76943
(325) 392-2022

Crosby County
201 West Aspen
Ste. 102
Crosbyton 79322
(806) 675-2334

Culberson County
Box 158
Van Horn 79855
(432) 283-2058

Dallam County
P.O. Box 1352
Dalhart 79022
(806) 244-4751

Dallas County
509 Main St.
Dallas 75202
(214) 653-7099

Dawson County
P.O. Box 1268
Lamesa 79331
(806) 872-3778

**Deaf Smith
County**
235 E. 3rd, Rm. 203
Hereford
79045-5542
(806) 363-7077

Delta County
200 W. Dallas Ave
Cooper 75432
(903) 395-4400

Denton County
1450 E. McKinney
Ste 1103
Denton 76209
(940) 349-2012

De Witt County
307 N. Gonzales St.
Cuero 77954
(361) 275-0864

Dickens County
P.O. Box 120
Dickens 79229
(806) 623-5531

Dimmit County
Courthouse
103 N. 5th St.
Carrizo Springs
78834
(830) 876-4209

Donley County
P.O. Drawer U
Clarendon 79226
(806) 874-3436

Duval County
P.O. Box 248
San Diego 78384
(361) 279-3322

Eastland County
P.O. Box 110
Eastland 76448
(254) 629-1583

Ector County
300 N. Grant
Room 111
Odessa 79761
(432) 498-4130

Edwards County
P.O. Box 184
Rocksprings 78880
(830) 683-2235

Ellis County
P.O. Box 250
Waxahachie 75168
(972) 923-5070

El Paso County
500 E. San Antonio
Rm 105
El Paso 79901
(915) 546-2071

Erath County
100 W. Washington
Stephenville 76401
(254) 965-1482

Falls County
P.O. Box 458
Marlin 76661
(254) 883-1408

Fannin County
101 E. Sam
Rayburn, #102
Bonham 75418
(903) 583-7488

Fayette County
P.O. Box 59
La Grange 78945
(979) 968-3251

Fisher County
P.O. Box 368
Roby 79543
(325) 776-2401

Floyd County
100 Main, Room 101
Floydada 79235
(806) 983-4900

Foard County
P.O. Box 539
Crowell 79227
(940) 684-1365

Fort Bend County
301 Jackson St.
Richmond 77469
(281) 341-8685

Franklin County
200 N. Kaufman St.
Mt. Vernon 75457
(903) 537-4252

Freestone County
P.O. Box 1010
Fairfield 75840
(903) 389-2635

Frio County
500 E. San
Antonio St., #6
Pearsall 78061
(830) 334-2214

Gaines County
101 So. Main,
Room 107
Seminole 79360
(432) 758-4033

Galveston County
P.O. Box 17253
Galveston
77552-7253
(409) 766-2210

Garza County
P.O. Box 366
Post 79356
(806) 495-4430

Gillespie County
101 West Main, #13
Fredericksburg
78624
(830) 997-6515

Glasscock County
P.O. Box 190
Garden City 79739
(432) 354-2371

Goliad County
P.O. Box 50
Goliad 77963
(361) 645-3294

Gonzales County
P.O. Box 77
Gonzales 78629
(830) 672-2801

Gray County
P.O. Box 1902
Pampa 79065
(806) 669-8004

Grayson County
100 W. Houston
Ste. 17
Sherman 75090
(903) 813-4235

Gregg County
P.O. Box 3049
Longview 75606
(903) 236-8430

Grimes County
P.O. Box 209
Anderson 77830
(936) 873-2111

Guadalupe County
101 E. Court St.
#206
Seguin 78155
(830) 303-4188

Hale County
500 Broadway #140
Plainview 79072
(806) 291-5205

Hall County
512 Main Street
Ste. 8
Memphis 79245
(806) 259-2627

Hamilton County
102 N. Rice St.
Suite 107
Hamilton 76531
(254) 386-3518

Hansford County
15 NW Court
Spearman 79081
(806) 659-4110

Hardeman County
P.O. Box 30
Quanah 79252
(940) 663-2961

Hardin County
P.O. Box 38
Kountze 77625
(409) 246-5185

Harris County
P.O. Box 1148
Houston
77251-1148
(713) 755-6411

Harrison County
P.O. Box 1365
Marshall 75671
(903) 935-4858

Hartley County
P.O. Box Q
Channing 79018
(806) 235-3582

Haskell County
P.O. Box 725
Haskell 79521
(940) 864-2451

Hays County
137 N. Guadalupe
Street
San Marcos 78666
(512) 393-7330

Hemphill County
P.O. Box 867
Canadian 79014
(806) 323-6212

Henderson County
101 E. Tyler St.
Courthouse, Athens
75751
(903) 675-6140

Hidalgo County
P.O. Box 58
Edinburg 78540
(956) 318-2100

Hill County
P.O. Box 398
Hillsboro 76645
(254) 582-4030

Hockley County
802 Houston
Ste. 213
Levelland 79336
(806) 894-3185

Hood County
P.O. Box 339
Granbury 76048
(817) 579-3222

Hopkins County
128 Jefferson St.
Ste. C
Sulphur Springs
75482
(903) 438-4074

Houston County
P.O. Box 370
Crockett 75835
(936) 544-3255

Howard County
P.O. Box 1468
Big Spring 79721
(432) 264-2213

Hudspeth County
P.O. Box 58
Sierra Blanca 79851
(915) 369-2301

Hunt County
P.O. Box 1316
Greenville 75403
(903) 408-4130

Hutchinson County
P.O. Box 1186
Stinnett 79083
(806) 878-4002

Irion County
P.O. Box 736
Mertzon 76941
(325) 835-2421

Jack County
100 Main, Ste 208
Jacksboro 76458
(940) 567-2111

Jackson County
115 W. Main
Rm. 101
Edna 77957
(361) 782-3563

Jasper County
P.O. Box 2070
Jasper 75951
(409) 384-2632

Jeff Davis County
P.O. Box 398
Fort Davis 79734
(432) 426-3251

Jefferson County
P.O. Box 1151
Beaumont 77704
(409) 835-8475

Jim Hogg County
P.O. Box 878
Hebbronville 78361
(361) 527-4031

Jim Wells County
P.O. Box 1459
Alice 78332
(361) 668-5702

Johnson County
P.O. Box 1986
Cleburne 76033
(817) 556-6312

Jones County
P.O. Box 552
Anson 79501
(325) 823-3762

Karnes County
101 N. Panna
Maria Ave.
Karnes City 78118
(830) 780-3938

Kaufman County
100 W. Mulberry St.
Kaufman 75142
(972) 932-4331

Kendall County
201 E. San Antonio
St., Ste. 127
Boerne 78006
(830) 249-9343

Kenedy County
P.O. Box 227
Sarita 78385
(361) 294-5220

Kent County
P.O. Box 9
Jayton 79528
(806) 237-3881

Kerr County
700 Main St.
Suite 122
Kerrville 78028
(830) 792-2255

Kimble County
501 Main St.
Junction 76849
(325) 446-3353

King County
P.O. Box 135
Guthrie 79236
(806) 596-4412

Kinney County
P.O. Box 9
Brackettville 78832
(830) 563-2521

Kleberg County
P.O. Box 1327
Kingsville 78364
(361) 595-8548

Knox County
P.O. Box 196
Benjamin 79505
(940) 459-2441

Lamar County
119 N. Main
Paris 75460
(903) 737-2420

Lamb County
100 6th Drive
Room 103
Littlefield 79339
(806) 385-4222

Lampasas County
P.O. Box 347
Lampasas 76550
(512) 556-8271

La Salle County
Courthouse Square
Ste 107
Cotulla 78014
(830) 879-4432

Lavaca County
P.O. Box 326
Hallettsville 77964
(361) 798-3612

Lee County
P.O. Box 419
Giddings 78942
(979) 542-3684

Leon County
P.O. Box 98
Centerville 75833
(903) 536-2352

Liberty County
P.O. Box 369
Liberty 77575
(936) 336-4670

Limestone County
200 W. State Street,
Ste 102
Groesbeck 76642
(254) 729-5504

Lipscomb County
P.O. Box 70
Lipscomb 79056
(806) 862-3091

Live Oak County
P.O. Box 280
George West 78022
(361) 449-2733

Llano County
P.O. Box 40
Llano 78643
(325) 247-4455

Loving County
P.O. Box 194
Mentone 79754
(432) 377-2441

Lubbock County
P.O. Box 10536
Lubbock 79408
(806) 775-1630

Lynn County
P.O. Box 937
Tahoka 79373
(806) 561-4750

Madison County
101 W. Main
Rm. 102
Madisonville 77864
(936) 348-2638

Marion County
P.O. Box 763
Jefferson 75657
(903) 665-3971

Martin County
Box 906
Stanton 79782
(432) 756-3412

Mason County
P.O. Box 702
Mason 76856
(325) 347-5253

Matagorda County
1700 Seventh St.
Room 202
Bay City 77414-5094
(979) 244-7680

Maverick County
500 Quarry Street
Suite 2
Eagle Pass 78852
(830) 773-2829

McCulloch County
101 N. High St.
Brady 76825
(325) 597-0733

McLennan County
P.O. Box 1727
Waco 76703
(254) 757-5078

McMullen County
P.O. Box 235
Tilden 78072
(361) 274-3215

Medina County
1100 16th St.
Rm. 109
Hondo 78861
(830) 741-6040

Menard County
P.O. Box 1038
Menard 76859
(325) 396-4682

Midland County
200 W. Wall
Suite 104
Midland 79701
(432) 688-1071

Milam County
107 W. Main
Cameron 76520
(254) 697-7049

Mills County
P.O. Box 646
Goldthwaite 76844
(325) 648-2711

Mitchell County
349 Oak St.
Rm. 103
Colorado City 79512
(325) 728-3481

Montague County
P.O. Box 77
Montague 76251
(940) 894-2461

Montgomery County
210 W. Davis
Suite 100
Conroe 77301
(936) 760-6941

Moore County
715 S. Dumas Ave.
Rm. 107
Dumas 79029
(806) 935-6164

Morris County
500 Broadnax
Street
Daingerfield 75638
(903) 645-3911

Motley County
P.O. Box 660
Matador 79244
(806) 347-2621

Nacogdoches County
101 W. Main St.,
Rm 205
Nacogdoches
75961
(936) 560-7733

Navarro County
P.O. Box 423
Corsicana 75151
(903) 654-3035

Newton County
P.O. Box 484
Newton 75966
(409) 379-5341

Nolan County
100 E. 3rd
Suite 108
Sweetwater 79556
(325) 235-2462

Nueces County
P.O. Box 2627
Corpus Christi
78403
(361) 888-0580

Ochiltree County
511 S. Main
Perryton 79070
(806) 435-8039

Oldham County
P.O. Box 360
Vega 79092
(806) 267-2667

Orange County
123 South 6th
Street
Orange 77630
(409) 882-7055

Palo Pinto County
P.O. Box 219
Palo Pinto 76484
(940) 659-1277

Panola County
110 S. Sycamore St.
Carthage 75633
(903) 693-0302

Parker County
P.O. Box 819
Weatherford 76086
(817) 594-7461

Parmer County
P.O. Box 356
Farwell 79325
(806) 481-3691

Pecos County
103 W. Callaghan
Fort Stockton 79735
(432) 336-7555

Polk County
P.O. Drawer 2119
Livingston 77351
(936) 327-6804

Potter County
P.O. Box 9638
Amarillo 79105
(806) 379-2275

Presidio County
P.O. Box 789
Marfa 79843
(432) 729-4812

Rains County
P.O. Box 187
Emory 75440
(903) 474-9999

Randall County
P.O. Box 660
Canyon 79015
(806) 468-5505

Reagan County
P.O. Box 100
Big Lake 76932
(325) 884-2442

Real County
P.O. Box 750
Leakey 78873
(830) 232-5202

Red River County
200 N. Walnut
Clarksville 75426
(903) 427-2401

Reeves County
P.O. Box 867
Pecos 79772
(432) 445-5467

Refugio County
P.O. Box 736
Refugio 78377
(361) 526-2233

Roberts County
P.O. Box 477
Miami 79059
(806) 868-2341

Robertson County
P.O. Box 1029
Franklin 77856
(979) 828-4130

Rockwall County
1101 Ridge Road
S-101
Rockwall 75087
(972) 882-0220

Runnels County
P.O. Box 189
Ballinger 76821
(325) 365-2720

Rusk County
115 North Main
Street #206
Henderson 75652
(903) 657-0330

Sabine County
P.O. Box 580
Hemphill 75948
(409) 787-3786

San Augustine Co.
100 W. Columbia,
Room 106
San Augustine
75972
(936) 275-2452

San Jacinto County
1 State Hwy 150,
Rm. 2
Coldspring 77331
(936) 653-2324

San Patricio County
P.O. Box 578
Sinton 78387
(361) 364-6290

San Saba County
500 E. Wallace
San Saba 76877
(325) 372-3614

Schleicher County
P.O. Drawer 580
Eldorado 76936
(325) 853-2833

Scurry County
1806 25th St.
Ste. 300
Snyder 79549
(325) 573-5332

Shackelford County
P.O. Box 247
Albany 76430
(325) 762-2232

Shelby County
P.O. Box 1987
Center 75935
(936) 598-6361

Sherman County
P.O. Box 270
Stratford 79084
(806) 366-2371

Smith County
P.O. Box 1018
Tyler 75710
(903) 590-4670

Somervell County
P.O. Box 1098
Glen Rose 76043
(254) 897-4427

Starr County
401 N. Britton Ave.,
Rm. 201
Rio Grande City
78582
(956) 487-8032

Stephens County
200 W. Walker
Breckenridge 76424
(254) 559-3700

Sterling County
P.O. Box 55
Sterling City 76951
(325) 378-5191

Stonewell County
P.O. Drawer P
Aspermont 79502
(940) 989-2272

Sutton County
300 E. Oak, Ste. 3
Sonora 76950
(325) 387-3815

Swisher County
119 S. Maxwell
Tulia 79088
(806) 995-3294

Tarrant County
100 W. Weatherford
Fort Worth 76196
(817) 884-1070

Taylor County
300 Oak St.
Abilene 79602
(325) 674-1205

Terrell County
P.O. Drawer 410
Sanderson 79848
(432) 345-2391

Terry County
500 W. Main
Rm. 105
Brownfield 79316
(806) 637-8551

Throckmorton County
P.O. Box 309
Throckmorton
76483
(940) 849-2501

Titus County
100 W. 1st, Ste. 204
Mt. Pleasant 75455
(903) 577-6796

Tom Green County
124 W. Beauregard
San Angelo 76903
(325) 659-6553

Travis County
P.O. Box 149325
Austin 78714-9325
(512) 854-4996

Trinity County
P.O. Box 456
Groveton 75845
(936) 642-1208

Tyler County
100 W. Bluff
Room 110
Woodville 75979
(409) 283-2281

Upshur County
P.O. Box 730
Gilmer 75644
(903) 843-4015

Upton County
P.O. Box 465
Rankin 79778
(432) 693-2861

Uvalde County
P.O. Box 284
Uvalde 78802-0284
(830) 278-6614

Val Verde County
P.O. Box 1267
Del Rio 78841-1267
(830) 774-7564

Van Zandt County
121 E. Dallas
Rm. 202
Canton 75103
(903) 567-6503

Victoria County
P.O. Box 1968
Victoria 77902
(361) 575-1478

Walker County
P.O. Box 210
Huntsville 77342
(936) 436-4922

Waller County
836 Austin St.
Rm. 103
Hempstead 77445
(979) 826-7643

Ward County
400 South Allen St.
Ste. 101
Monahans 79756
(432) 943-3294

Washington County
100 E. Main
Suite 102
Brenham 77833
(979) 277-6200

Webb County
1110 Victoria St.
#201
Laredo 78040
(956) 523-4265

Wharton County
309 E. Milam
Ste 700
Wharton 77488
(979) 532-2381

Wheeler County
Box 465
Wheeler 79096
(806) 826-5544

Wichita County
P.O. Box 1679
Wichita Falls
76307-1679
(940) 766-8144

Wilbarger County
1700 Wilbarger St.
Rm. 15
Vernon 76384
(940) 552-5486

Willacy County
576 W. Main
Raymondville
78580
(956) 689-2710

Williamson County
405 MLK, Box 14
Georgetown 78626
(512) 943-1515

Wilson County
P.O. Box 27
Floresville 78114
(830) 393-7308

Winkler County
P.O. Box 1007
Kermit 79745
(432) 586-3401

Wise County
P.O. Box 359
Decatur 76234
(940) 627-3351

Wood County
P.O. Box 1796
Quitman 75783
(903) 763-2711

Yoakum County
P.O. Box 309
Plains 79355
(806) 456-2721

Young County
516 Fourth St.,
Room 104
Graham 76450
(940) 549-8432

Zapata County
P.O. Box 789
Zapata 78076
(956) 765-9915

Zavala County
200 E. Uvalde St.
Ste 7
Crystal City 78839
(830) 374-2331

Bureaus of Vital Statistics

Texas Notaries are not permitted to make certified copies of any document that is recordable or a public record. Persons requesting "notarization," "certification" or certified copies of birth or death certificates should be referred to the appropriate public office. The following state agencies can provide certified copies of birth and death records of persons who were born or have died in the respective states, as can certain local offices not listed here:

Alabama
Vital Records
Department of Public Health
P.O. Box 5625
Montgomery, AL 36103-5625

Alaska
Bureau of Vital Statistics
Department of Health &
Social Services
5441 Commercial Blvd.
P.O. Box 110675
Juneau, AK 99801

Arizona
Office of Vital Records
Department of Health Services
P.O. Box 3887
Phoenix, AZ 85030-3887

Arkansas
Division of Vital Records
Department of Health
4815 West Markham Street, Slot 44
Little Rock, AR 72205-3867

California
Office of Vital Records
Department of Health Services
P.O. Box 997410, MS: 5103
Sacramento, CA 95899-7410

Colorado
Vital Records Section
Department of Health
4300 Cherry Creek Drive South
Denver, CO 80246-1530

Connecticut
Department of Public Health
State Office of Vital Records
410 Capitol Avenue, MS #11VRS
P.O. Box 340308
Hartford, CT 06134-0308

Delaware
Health Statistics Center
Office of Vital Statistics
Jesse S. Cooper Building
417 Federal Street
Dover, DE 19901

District of Columbia
Vital Records Division
825 North Capitol Street NE
1st Floor
Washington, DC 20002

Florida
Office of Vital Statistics
1217 Pearl Street
P.O. Box 210
Jacksonville, FL 32231

Georgia
Vital Records
2600 Skyland Drive NE
Atlanta, GA 30319-3640

Hawaii
Vital Statistics Section
State Department of Health
P.O. Box 3378
Honolulu, HI 96801

Idaho
Vital Statistics Unit
450 West State Street, 1st Floor
P.O. Box 83720
Boise, ID 83720-0036

Illinois
Division of Vital Records
Department of Public Health
605 West Jefferson Street
Springfield, IL 62702-5097

Indiana
Vital Records Department
State Department of Health
6 West Washington Street
Indianapolis, IN 46204

Iowa
Department of Public Health
Bureau of Vital Records
Lucas Office Building, 1st Floor
321 East 12th Street
Des Moines, IA 50319-0075

Kansas
Office of Vital Statistics
1000 SW Jackson Street, Suite 120
Topeka, KS 66612-2221

Kentucky
Office of Vital Statistics
Department for Health Services
275 East Main Street, 1E-A
Frankfort, KY 40621-0001

Louisiana
Vital Records Registry
P.O. Box 60630
New Orleans, LA 70160

Maine
Vital Statistics
221 State Street
11 State House Station
Augusta, ME 04333-0011

Maryland
Division of Vital Records
Department of Health
6550 Reisterstown Road
Baltimore, MD 21215

Massachusetts
Registry of Vital Records and
Statistics
150 Mount Vernon Street, 1st Floor
Dorchester, MA 02125-3105

Michigan
Vital Records Request
P.O. Box 30721
Lansing, MI 48909

Minnesota
Department of Health
Office of the State Registrar
P.O. Box 64882
St. Paul, MN 55164-0882

Mississippi
Vital Records
P.O. Box 1700
Jackson, MS 39215-1700

Missouri
Department of Health
Bureau of Vital Records
930 Wildwood
P.O. Box 570
Jefferson City, MO 65102-0570

Montana
Office of Vital Statistics
P.O. Box 4210
111 North Sanders, Room 209
Helena, MT 59604

Nebraska
Vital Statistics
Department of Health
301 Centennial Mall South
P.O. Box 95065
Lincoln, NE 68509-5065

Nevada
Office of Vital Records
4150 Technology Way, Suite 104
Carson City, NV 89706

New Hampshire
Department of State
Division of Vital Records
Administration
71 South Fruit Street
Concord, NH 03301-2410

New Jersey
Vital Statistics
Customer Service
P.O. Box 370
Trenton, NJ 08625-0370

New Mexico
Vital Records and Health Statistics
1105 St. Francis Drive
Santa Fe, NM 87502

New York
State Department of Health
Vital Records Section
Certification Unit
P.O. Box 2602
Albany, NY 12220-2602

New York City
Office of Vital Records
New York City Department
of Health
125 Worth Street, CN4, Room 133
New York, NY 10013

North Carolina
Vital Records
1903 Mail Service Center
Raleigh, NC 27699-1903

North Dakota
Division of Vital Records
600 East Boulevard Avenue,
Dept. 301
Bismarck, ND 58505-0200

Ohio
Department of Health
Vital Statistics
P.O. Box 15098
Columbus, OH 43215-0098

Oklahoma
Vital Records Service
State Department of Health
1000 Northeast 10th Street
Oklahoma City, OK 73117

Oregon
Vital Records
P.O. Box 14050
Portland, OR 97293-0050

Pennsylvania
Division of Vital Records
101 South Mercer Street, Room 401
P.O. Box 1528
New Castle, PA 16101

Rhode Island
Office of Vital Records
Department of Health
3 Capitol Hill Road, Room 101
Providence, RI 02908-5097

South Carolina
Office of Vital Records
South Carolina DHEC
2600 Bull Street
Columbia, SC 29201

South Dakota
Vital Records
207 East Missouri Avenue, Suite #1A
Pierre, SD 57501

Tennessee
Vital Records
Central Services Building
421 5th Avenue North
Nashville, TN 37247

Texas
Bureau of Vital Statistics
Department of Health
P.O. Box 12040
Austin, TX 78711-2040

Utah
Vital Records and Statistics
Cannon Health Building
288 North 1460 West
P.O. Box 141012
Salt Lake City, UT 84114-1012

Vermont
Department of Health
Vital Records Section
108 Cherry Street
P.O. Box 70
Burlington, VT 05402-0070

Virginia
Office of Vital Records
P.O. Box 1000
Richmond, VA 23218-1000

Washington
Department of Health
Center for Health Statistics
P.O. Box 9709
Olympia, WA 98507-9709

West Virginia
Vital Registration Office
350 Capitol Street, Room 165
Charleston, WV 25301-3701

Wisconsin
Vital Records
1 West Wilson Street
P.O. Box 309
Madison, WI 53701-0309

Wyoming
Vital Records Services
Hathaway Building
Cheyenne, WY 82002

American Samoa
Office of Records and Vital Statistics
LBJ Tropical Medical Center
Department of Health Services
American Samoa Government
Pago Pago, AS 96799

Guam
Office of Vital Statistics
Department of Public Health
P.O. Box 2816
Agana, GU, M.I. 96910

Northern Mariana Islands
Bureau of Health Planning
Statistics Office
P.O. Box 500409 CK
Saipan, MP 96950-0409

Panama Canal Zone
Vital Records Section
Passport Services
U.S. Department of State
1111 19th Street NW, Suite 510
Washington, DC 20522-1705

Puerto Rico
Department of Health
Demographic Registry
P.O. Box 11854
Fernández Juncos Station
San Juan, PR 00910

Virgin Islands (St. Croix)
Department of Health
Vital Statistics
Charles Harwood Memorial Hospital
St. Croix, VI 00820

Virgin Islands
(St. Thomas, St. John)
Department of Health
Registrar of Vital Statistics
Knud Hansen Complex
St. Thomas, VI 00802

Hague Convention Nations

The nations listed on the following pages are parties to a treaty called the *Hague Convention Abolishing the Requirement of Legalization [Authentication] for Foreign Public Documents*, hereafter simply called the Hague Convention.

Treaty Simplifies Authentication. A Notary's signature on documents that are sent to these nations may be authenticated (verified as valid for the benefit of the recipient in the foreign nation) through attachment of a single authenticating certificate called an *apostille*. The *apostille* (French for "notation") is the only authenticating certificate necessary. Nations not subscribing to the Hague Convention may require as many as five or six separate authenticating certificates from different governmental agencies, domestic and foreign.

How to Request an *Apostille*. An *apostille* may be obtained through mail or in person at the following address. To request an *apostille* by mail, send the notarized document with a written request indicating the country to which the document will be sent, a self-addressed, stamped envelope and a $5 check payable to the "TX Secretary of State," to:

Street Address:
Secretary of State
Notary Public Unit
1019 Brazos
Austin, TX 78701

Mailing Address:
Secretary of State
Notary Public Unit
P.O. Box 13375
Austin, TX 78711-3375

An *apostille* must be specifically requested, and the nation to which the document will be sent must be indicated. It is not the

Notary's responsibility to obtain an *apostille*; it is the responsibility of the party needing authentication.

Hague Convention Nations. The nations listed below participate in the Hague Convention. Footnotes reflect information most likely to be of interest to Notaries acting in the United States and its territories. Please note that some nations listed may not recognize the participation of every other nation listed. To verify recognition between nations, consult the Web site of the Hague Conference on Private International Law at http://www.hcch.net/index_en.php.

Albania
Andorra[13]
Antigua and Barbuda[13]
Argentina[1]
Armenia[13]
Australia
Austria
Azerbaijan[13]
Bahamas[13]
Barbados[13]
Belarus
Belgium[7]
Belize[13]
Bosnia and Herzegovina[2]
Botswana[13]
Brunei Darussalam[13]
Bulgaria
Colombia[13]
Cook Islands[13]
Croatia[2]
Cyprus
Czech Republic
Denmark[3]
Dominica[13]
Dominican
  Republic[13]
Ecuador
El Salvador[13]
Estonia
Fiji[13]
Finland
France[4]
Georgia[5]
Germany[7]
Greece

Grenada[13]
Honduras[13]
Hong Kong[6]
Hungary
Iceland
India
Ireland
Israel
Italy
Japan
Kazakhstan[13]
Latvia
Lesotho[13]
Liberia[7,13]
Liechtenstein[13]
Lithuania
Luxembourg
Macao[6]
Macedonia[2]
Malawi[13]
Malta
Marshall Islands[13]
Mauritius[13]
Mexico
Moldova[13]
Monaco
Montenegro[2]
Namibia[13]
Netherlands[8]
New Zealand[9]
Niue[13]
North Korea
Norway
Panama
Poland

Portugal[10]
Romania
Russian
  Federation
Saint Kitts and
  Nevis[13]
Saint Lucia[13]
Saint Vincent
  and the
  Grenadines[13]
Samoa[13]
San Marino[13]
Sao Tome e
  Principe[13]
Serbia[2]
Seychelles[13]
Slovakia

Slovenia[2]
South Africa
Spain
Suriname
Swaziland[13]
Sweden
Switzerland
Tonga[13]
Trinidad and Tobago[13]
Turkey
Ukraine
United
  Kingdom[1,11]
United States[7,12]
Vanuatu[13]
Venezuela

Inquiries. Persons having questions about the *Hague Convention Abolishing the Requirement of Legalization for Foreign Public Documents* may address their inquiries to:

> Authentication Office
> 518 23rd Street, NW
> State Annex 1
> Washington, DC 20037
> (202) 647-5002

---

1. Argentina does not recognize the extension of the Convention by the United Kingdom to the Malvinas (Falkland Islands), South Georgia, South Sandwich Islands and the Argentine Antarctic Sector (British Antarctic Territory). See n. 11.
2. The former Socialist Federal Republic of Yugoslavia was a party to the Convention. Only the successor states of Bosnia and Herzegovina, Croatia, the Republic of Macedonia, Montenegro, Serbia and Slovenia have confirmed that the Convention still applies.
3. The participation of Denmark does not extend to Greenland and the Faro Islands.
4. The participation of France is extended to the entire territory of the French Republic, including French Guyana, French Polynesia, Guadeloupe, Martinique, Mayotte, New Caledonia, Reunion, St. Barthelemy, St. Martin, St. Pierre and Miquelon, and Wallis and Futuna.
5. The participation of Georgia does not extend to Abkhazia and South Ossetia.
6. Hong Kong and Macao retained their status as Hague nations after control was returned to China on July 1, 1997 (Hong Kong) and December 20, 1999 (Macao).
7. The participation of New Zealand does not extend to Tokelau.
8. The Convention does not apply between Liberia and the United States, Belgium or Germany.
9. The participation of the Netherlands is extended to Aruba and the Netherlands Antilles.
10. The participation of Portugal is extended to the entire territory of the Republic of Portugal, including the Azores and Madeira.
11. The participation of the United Kingdom of Great Britain and Northern Ireland is extended to Anguilla, Bermuda, British Antarctic Territory, British Virgin Islands, Cayman Islands, Falkland Islands, Gibraltar, Guernsey, Isle of Man, Jersey, Montserrat, St. Helena and Turks and Caicos Islands.
12. The United States includes American Samoa, District of Columbia, Guam, Northern Mariana Islands, Puerto Rico and U.S. Virgin Islands.
13. This nation is not a member of the Hague Conference on Private International Law but is a party to the Hague Convention Abolishing the Requirement of Legalization for Foreign Public Documents.

About
the NNA

Since 1957, the National Notary Association — a nonprofit educational organization — has served the nation's Notaries Public with a wide variety of instructional programs and services.

As the country's clearinghouse for information on Notary laws, customs and practices, the NNA educates Notaries through publications, seminars, webinars, online training, annual conferences, its website and a Notary Information Service Hotline that offers immediate answers to specific questions about notarization.

The Association is perhaps most widely known as the preeminent source of information for and about Notaries. NNA works include the following:

- *The National Notary*, a magazine for NNA members featuring how-to articles and practical tips on notarizing

- *Notary Bulletin*, an eNewsletter that keeps NNA members and customers up to date on developments affecting Notaries, especially new state laws and regulations

- *Sorry, No Can Do!* series, four volumes that help Notaries explain to customers and bosses why some requests for notarizations are improper and cannot be accommodated

- *U.S. Notary Reference Manual*, an invaluable resource for any person relying upon the authenticity and correctness of legal documents

- *Notary Public Practices & Glossary*, a definitive reference book on notarial procedures and widely hailed as the Notary's bible

- *State Notary Law Primers*, short guidebooks that explain a state's Notary statutes in easy-to-understand language

- *The Notary Public Code of Professional Responsibility*, a comprehensive and detailed code of ethical and professional conduct for Notaries

- *The Model Notary Act*, prototype legislation conceived in 1973 and updated in 1984, 2002 and 2010 by an NNA-recruited panel of secretaries of state, legislators and attorneys, and regularly used by state legislatures in revising their Notary laws

- *Notary Law & Practice: Cases & Materials*, the definitive and one-of-a-kind text for teaching Notary law to law students in schools and to attorneys in Minimum Continuing Education Seminars (MCLE), discussing every major judicial decision affecting the Notary's duties

- *Notary Signing Agent Training Course*, a manual covering every aspect of signing agent procedures that prepares candidates for the Notary Signing Agent Certification Examination developed by the NNA

- Public-service pamphlets informing the general public about the function of a Notary, including *What Is A Notary Public?* printed in English and Spanish

In addition, the NNA offers the highest quality professional supplies, including official seals and stamps, embossers, recordkeeping journals, jurat stamps, thumbprinting devices and notarial certificates.

Though dedicated primarily to educating and assisting Notaries, the NNA devotes part of its resources to helping lawmakers draft effective Notary statutes and to informing the public about the Notary's vital role in modern society. ■

Index

Page numbers listed in **bold** indicate where the most complete information on a subject can be found. *Italics* indicate the pages where the statutes pertaining to a subject are located.

Page numbers listed in **bold** indicate where the most complete information on a subject can be found. *Italics* indicate the pages where the statutes pertaining to a subject are located.

BEFORE YOU NOTARIZE —
BE PREPARED WITH THE NNA.

ou are thinking of becoming a
tary or are a veteran, the National
tary Association is your best
ource for training and support!
ey are committed to you…
— **Nancy R., Bakersfield, CA**

horough knowledge of your state's statutes and standard
ocedures is essential to performing error-free signings.
hether you need state-required training or desire to
prove your skills and proficiency, the NNA has the
aining you want to suit your needs.

- Online Courses
- Self-Study Books
- Annual Conference
- Webinars

THE LEADER IN NOTARY TRAINING SINCE 1957.
earn more at NationalNotary.org/Training

2 National Notary Association

Source Code
A46151

THERE FOR YOU DURING YOUR NOTARY COMMISSION.

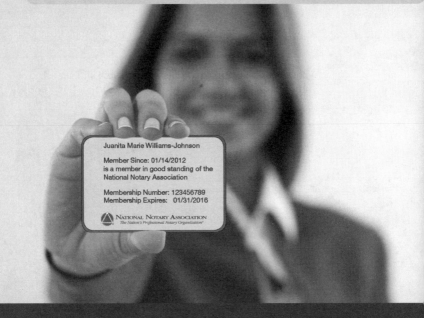

Juanita Marie Williams-Johnson

Member Since: 01/14/2012
is a member in good standing of the
National Notary Association

Membership Number: 123456789
Membership Expires: 01/31/2016

NATIONAL NOTARY ASSOCIATION
The Nation's Professional Notary Organization®

Becoming a member of the NNA means you've chosen a path
enhance your career and better serve your customers. You ha
separated yourself as a Notary committed to advanced educatic
the highest levels of professional standards and superior custom
service. Valuable benefits, support and networking opportunit
are yours when you join today.

- **Unlimited access to our toll-free Notary Hotline** — there
  for you when you need a tough notarization question
  answered quickly.

- **Weekly newsletters and bi-monthly magazine** featuring
  the latest industry updates.

- **Exclusive member-only discount pricing** on education,
  supplies, bonds, and E&O insurance.

- **Personal and professional growth opportunities** through
  high-quality education and training resources.

Join today by visiting
NationalNotary.org/Join

Source
A46

TESTED. TRUSTED.

Quality Notary Supplies From the NNA

As the nation's leading provider of Notary products, the NNA h
the professional tools you need to perform or prepare for yo
official duties. Made from the highest quality materials, all produc
meet state requirements and are guaranteed to last. Choose from

Journals and Thumbprinters	**Notary Certificates**
Seal Stamps	**Reference Books**
Embossers	**Training**

And much more

To order visit
**NationalNotary.org/supplies or
call 1-888-896-6827**

Source C
A461